HOT DOG!

ANDY LYNES

PORTICO

First published in the United Kingdom in 2015 by
Portico
1 Gower Street
London
WC1E 6HD

An imprint of Pavilion Books Company Ltd

ISBN 978-1-910496-62-6

A CIP catalogue record for this book is available from
the British Library.

10 9 8 7 6 5 4 3 2 1

Reproduction by Mission Productions Ltd, Hong Kong
Printed and bound by 1010 Printing International, Ltd

This book can be ordered direct from the publisher
at www.pavilionbooks.com

Illustrations by Andy @ KJA Artists

CONTENTS

INTRODUCTION 4
THE HISTORY OF HOT DOGS 6
Currywurst 9
HOT DOGS IN AMERICA 10
REGIONAL AMERICAN DOGS 12
Chicago Hot Dog 16
Philly Cheese Dog 17
Sloppy Joe Dog 18
Chilli Cheese Dog 19
WHAT'S IN YOUR HOT DOG? 20
Corn Dog 22
Po' Boy 23
THE RISE OF THE 'HAUTE DOG' 24

WORLD'S WEIRDEST HOT DOGS 26
Korean Kimchi Dog 30
Spanish Dog 31
Malaysian Satay Dog 32
Mexican Hot Dog Wrap 33
HOT DOGS ON THE SCREEN 34
HOT DOG SONGS 36
Thai Dog 40
Indian Chapati Hot Dog Wrap 41
Middle Eastern Hot Dog 42
Sunday Roast Dog 44
HOT DOG HUMOUR 46
HOT DOG QUIZ 48
BBQ Dog with Pulled Pork 52
Blue Cheese and Bacon Dog 53
Pizza Dog 54
HOT DOG TRIVIA 55
10 FAMOUS HOT DOG RESTAURANTS 56
KNOW YOUR BUNS 58
Hot Dog Buns 60
Brioche Hot Dog Buns 62
Pretzel Hot Dog Buns 63
HOT DOG EATING COMPETITIONS 64

WITH RELISH! (RELISHES, TOPPINGS & SIDES) 66
Ketchup 70
Yellow Mustard 71
Mayonnaise, Three Ways 72
Sweet Pickle Relish 74
Maple Mustard Sauce 75
Caramelized Onions 78
New York Onions 78
Crispy Shallots 79
Coleslaw 80
Asian Slaw 81
Remoulade 82
Cucumber Pickles 83
MAKING A MEAL OF YOUR HOT DOG 84
Skin-On Fries 88
Chilli Cheese Fries 89
Bacon Ranch Fries 90
Potato Salad 91
Potato Knish 92
Onion Rings 93
Hot Dog Mac 'n' Cheese 94
Poutine 95
HOT DOGS A–Z 96

INTRODUCTION

Hot dogs are one of the most popular and familiar finger foods in the world. As you'll learn from reading this book, their invention is steeped in myth and mystery, as is the reason they acquired their frankly bizarre name. (Ever smelled a real hot dog? The last thing the aroma of an overheated Labrador will make you is hungry.) But despite the hazy origins and odd nomenclature, hot dogs are one of America's greatest culinary gifts to the world.

With 40 fun and tasty recipes, this book provides you with everything you'll need for an authentic hot dog experience, apart from a New York street or baseball stadium to eat it in, that is. You'll learn not only how to prepare a classic American-style hot dog, but also how to reinvent a dog as a true gastronomic treat with culinary ideas drawn from around the globe. By using the range of relishes and toppings (see pages 66–83) you can create your own gourmet dogs, and by adding a few side dishes make a real meal out of them.

Once you've got the hot dog bug, why not hit the road and check out some of the finest hot dog restaurants around the world and see how the professionals do it (see pages 56–57), including some top chefs who've put their own stamp on the humble dog.

With billions sold around the world every year, hot dogs are big business. Turf wars between street vendors fighting over prime locations have sprung up in major cities around the world including London and New York. You can even go to Hot Dog University in Chicago and learn 'the art of the cart' and how to run your own stand or restaurant.

There are plenty of punters who take hot dogs very seriously; Google 'New York vs. Chicago hot dog' for a torrent of impassioned debate. There are even hot dog historians like Bruce Kraig, Ph.D., professor emeritus at Roosevelt University in Illinois, and etymologist and consulting editor of the *Oxford Encyclopaedia of Food and Drink* in America, Barry Popik.

But there is something inherently funny about a hot dog. Maybe it's the phallic shape, maybe it's that dumb name, or the fact that a hot dog sausage is called a 'wiener' in America, but hot dogs simply refuse to be taken too seriously. (For proof, check out Hot Dog Humour on pages 46–47.) In a world where food snobbery increasingly threatens to suck all the fun out of eating, that can only be a good thing.

THE HISTORY OF HOT DOGS

Hot dogs as we know them today, a sausage in a bun, were invented in the 1870s in Coney Island, Brooklyn, New York by seaside food vendor Charles Feltman. But it could have been a decade later by another Coney Island resident, Ignatz Frischman, who it's said was the first to realize that the popular frankfurter sausage sandwiches sold in the neighbourhood would make more sense served in a long bun.

But maybe it was in Chicago in 1893 at the World's Columbian Exposition, held to celebrate the 400th anniversary of Christopher Columbus's arrival in the New World. Or perhaps it was at the St. Louis Louisiana Purchase Exposition in 1904, when Anton Feuchtwanger asked his baker brother-in-law to come up with something to replace the gloves he loaned to his customers so they could hold the hot sausages, and which they never returned. Or was it was even earlier than all of that? Some say a German immigrant sold hot dogs from a push cart in the 1860s in the Bowery district of New York.

When it comes to hot dog history, there's plenty of it, it's just that no one seems to be able to agree on the precise facts. Perhaps the truth is that putting a sausage in a roll is such a simple notion that numerous people came up with it at different times, and it was only when hot dogs became hugely popular that anyone tried to lay claim to the snack food's invention.

The hot dog *sausage*'s origins go back much further than America in the 19th century, though. Vienna in Austria laid claim to its invention with a huge party in 1987 celebrating the 500th anniversary of the birth of the wiener or Vienna sausage. However the German city of Frankfurt could (and does) equally call itself the birthplace of the hot dog as it's home to the frankfurter sausage, also created in the 14th century.

The origins of the name hot dog have also been obscured by time. Tad Dorgan, a cartoonist on the *New York Journal*, was credited with coining the term when he reputedly drew a dachshund dog (the short-legged, long-bodied breed thought to have been brought to North America by the same immigrants who brought the wiener and frankfurter) in a roll and captioned it 'get your hot dogs' in the early 1900s. The only problem with the story is that, despite Dorgan's popularity, no one can find a copy of his cartoon in the archives of the prolific artist's work.

What historians *have* discovered is a reference in a 1895 copy of college magazine the *Yale Record* that described students who 'munched hot dogs' which were sold from carts outside the University dormitories. Those that indulged were dubbed the 'Kennel Club', and the term 'hot dog' is thought to be a poke at the dubious source of the meat the sausages were made from. They were probably joking, but the Coney Island Chamber of Commerce failed to see the funny side, and in 1913 forbade traders from using the words 'hot dog' on their signs. To this day, the National Hot Dog and Sausage Council (yes, there really is such a thing) say the most frequently asked question of them is 'what really goes into a hot dog?', although if there are still any reservations about the make-up of the sausage, it doesn't stop Americans eating about 20 billion of them a year.

GET YOUR HOT DOGS!

CURRYWURST

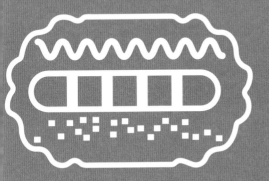

If you haven't tried this snack on the streets of Berlin or Cologne, you are in for a surprisingly delicious treat. Usually served as slices of fried Bratwurst sausage on a carton of chips, slathered in currywurst sauce, dusted with curry and chilli powders, this is the same thing, just served in a roll.

Serves 4

2 tbsp vegetable oil
1 onion, finely chopped
2 tbsp curry powder, plus more for dusting
200g/7oz/scant 1 cup passata
200g/7oz/scant 1 cup ketchup (see page 70)
1 tsp Worcestershire sauce
1 tsp sea salt
4 Bratwurst sausages
4 hot dog buns
4 tsp mild chilli powder

Heat half of the oil in a pan over medium heat and add the onion. Cook, stirring continuously, for 3 minutes until the onion is soft but not coloured. Add the curry powder and cook for a further minute, then add the passata, ketchup, Worcestershire sauce and salt and leave to simmer gently for 30 minutes. Check the seasoning and keep warm.

Heat the remaining oil in a frying pan and cook the sausages for 15 minutes until brown and cooked through. Slice the buns lengthways, put one sausage in each bun, top with the sauce and sprinkle over the curry powder and chilli powder. Serve with ketchup (see page 70), mayonnaise (see page 72) and skin-on fries (see page 88).

HOT DOGS IN AMERICA

Hot dogs are the world's favourite finger food. You'll find versions eaten all over the world from China to Moscow, but nowhere loves hot dogs more than America. In 2014, a billion packs of hot dogs were sold in American supermarkets. The US first fell in love with hot dogs in a major way in Coney Island in Brooklyn, where former hot dog-cart operator Charles Feltman built a mini-empire of hotel, beer gardens, restaurants, food stands and amusements in the late 19th and early 20th century, selling up to 40,000 hot dogs a day.

Other operators cashed in, creating work for immigrants who then spread out across the country, setting up their own businesses or simply inspiring others to do the same – like Greek immigrant James Mallis who, seeing the success of Nathan's Famous in Coney Island (see page 56), opened Nu-Way in Macon, Georgia in 1916.

Virtually the most American thing you can do is eat a hot dog at a baseball game. That over 21 million dogs are scoffed at ballparks every year is down to one man, Harry Stevens. Ironically, he wasn't born in New York or Chicago, but Derby in the north of England. Stevens arrived in Niles, Ohio in 1882, began publishing programmes for the local baseball game, and was soon producing them for the National League. Stevens started selling food alongside the programmes, and by 1894 had become a concessionaire at the famous Polo Grounds in Upper Manhattan (now demolished).

Stevens is the subject of one of many highly dubious 'origin of the hot dog' stories. It's said that one day in 1901 he ran out of stocks of ice cream and hard-boiled eggs and in a panic ordered sausages, and buns to hold them in, and called them Dachshund Sausages, which then became hot dogs (this highly disputed incident is meant to have inspired Tad Dorgan's cartoon (see page 8). Whatever the veracity of the story, Stevens contribution to the hot dog hasn't been forgotten, and he even has his own day dedicated to him in his adopted home town of Niles.

RED SNAPPER

CHICAGO DOG

NEW YORK DOG

SONORAN DOG

THE CONEY

THE HALF-SMOKE

REGIONAL AMERICAN DOGS

Contrary to popular belief, there isn't such a thing as a definitive American hot dog; there are many American dogs, each one a delicious iteration on one simple but brilliant idea. Subtle variations on relishes and toppings, type of sausage, buns and cooking methods create a dazzling gastronomic kaleidoscope of taste and texture. Come with us as we guide you through some of America's best regional dogs. Bring your appetite, you're going to need it.

New York
The most simple and elegant of all the regional variations, your dog will be grilled, served in a side-split bun and garnished simply with onions, either steamed or fried in a spicy tomato paste (see page 78) or sauerkraut, and ketchup or mustard.

Chicago
The yang to NYC's yin, there are so many elements to this dog that they say it has been 'dragged through the garden'. A steamed or simmered all-beef dog in a poppy seed bun comes loaded with tomato, hot peppers, dill pickle, chopped onions, yellow mustard, celery and a positively radioactive-looking neon-green sweet relish. See the recipe on page 16 for the full info.

Slaw Dog
This is an entire sub-category of hot dogs all to itself, but ask to go 'all the way' when you're in pretty much any Southern state and you'll get a dog topped with creamy coleslaw, chilli, onions and mustard. As long as you're at a hot dog stand when you ask, of course. Anywhere else and you might get a whole different answer. Or a slap.

The Sonoran Dog, Arizona
Named after neighbouring Sonora, Mexico. Grilled, bacon-wrapped hot dogs are placed in Mexican-style bolillo rolls (mini baguettes) and topped with pinto beans, tomatoes, onions, jalapeños and sour cream.

The Half-Smoke, Washington
The name refers to the sausage, a coarse-ground half-pork, half-beef, smoked sausage that's grilled or steamed, served in a steamed bun and topped with chilli con carne, mustard and chopped onions.

Red Snapper, Maine
In Chicago they like food colouring in their relish. In Maine, they prefer it in the natural casing of their beef and pork franks, which are dyed bright red, grilled and served in a toasted, top-split bun topped with mustard.

The Coney, Michigan
It's the chilli topping that really defines this particular variation. If you love offal then you'll go a bundle on the mildly spiced, meaty sauce that includes 'nasty bits' like beef heart and kidney.

CHICAGO HOT DOG

CHEESE DOG

SLOPPY JOE DOG

CHICAGO HOT DOG

For a truly authentic Chicago dog you'll need to track down sport peppers and neon-green relish, both of which are hard to come by outside of North America. However, any pickled green chilli makes a perfectly acceptable substitute for the peppers, and that neon glow is achieved with a flavourless food colouring, so its absence won't affect the flavour of your dog.

Makes 4 (ORDER UP! PAGE 14)

4 all-beef hot dogs
4 poppy seed hot dog buns, split lengthways
yellow mustard, to taste (see page 71)
4 tbsp sweet pickle relish (see page 74)
4 tbsp chopped white onions
1 large ripe tomato, cut into 8 wedges
4 cucumber pickles (see page 83) or dill pickle
8 pickled sport peppers, or any pickled chilli pepper of your choice
celery salt

Heat the hot dogs through in simmering water for 3 minutes or according to the manufacturer's instructions.

Put a hot dog in each of the buns and squeeze some mustard over each one. Top each dog with a tablespoon of the relish, followed by a tablespoon of onions. Arrange two tomato wedges along one side of the sausage and a cucumber pickle or dill pickle on the other. Top each dog with two pickled chillies and sprinkle over a pinch of celery salt.

PHILLY CHEESE DOG

The classic American sandwich Philly cheese steak was invented in Philadelphia in 1930 by brothers Pat and Harry M. Olivieri, who just happened to own a hot dog stand. So it made sense to adapt the sandwich, usually made with thin slices of griddled ribeye steak, fried onions and cheese sauce (and sometimes sautéed peppers and mushrooms), to a dog.

Makes 4 (ORDER UP! PAGE 15)

2 tbsp olive oil
500g/12lb 2oz/7½ cups button
    mushrooms, cleaned and sliced
1 onion, sliced
1 red (bell) pepper, deseeded and
    sliced
1 green (bell) pepper, deseeded and
    sliced
1 clove garlic, finely minced
1 tsp paprika
200ml/7fl oz/scant 1 cup cheese
    sauce (see page 94), warm
4 beef hot dogs
4 hot dog buns
ketchup (see page 70, optional)

Preheat the grill (broiler) to medium.

Heat half the oil in a pan and cook the mushrooms until all the moisture has evaporated. Transfer the mushrooms to a bowl and set aside.

Add the remaining oil to the pan and cook the onions and peppers over a medium heat, stirring occasionally until softened. Add the garlic and cook for 1 minute until it releases its aroma. Add the paprika and cook for 1 minute more. Return the mushrooms to the pan and reheat.

Place the hot dogs under the grill (broiler) for 3 minutes, or until cooked through. Place a hot dog in each bun, spoon over some of the peppers and mushrooms and top with the cheese sauce. Finish with the ketchup, if using. Serve with skin-on fries (see page 88) and onion rings (see page 93).

SLOPPY JOE DOG

There's some confusion over the exact origin of the sloppy Joe. Some say it originated in Cuba, others claim the loose meat sandwich was first served at a café in Iowa in 1930 by a chef named Joe. Often served as just the meat mixture in a hamburger bun, there are many variations, including a version from Quebec served in a hot dog bun. So why not go all the way and add the hot dog itself?

Serves 4 (ORDER UP! PAGE 15)

500g/1lb 2oz good-quality minced beef
1 tbsp vegetable oil
1 large onion, finely diced
1 stick celery, finely diced
1 clove garlic, crushed
1 tbsp tomato purée
1 tbsp muscovado sugar
1 red (bell) pepper, roasted, skinned, deseeded and chopped

400 g/14oz tin chopped tomatoes
1 tbsp tomato purée
1 tbsp muscovado sugar
2 tbsp ketchup (see page 70)
2 tbsp Worcestershire sauce
4 hot dog buns, split along the top
4 beef hot dogs
4 tbsp crispy shallots (see page 79)
sea salt and black pepper

Put a large, heavy-based pan over a high heat and add the beef. Break the beef down with a wooden spoon and cook in its own juices for 5 minutes until browned. Drain the meat in a fine colander and set aside.

Return the pan to the heat, reduce the heat to medium and add the oil. Add the onion and celery and cook, stirring continuously, for 5 minutes until softened. Add the garlic and cook for 1 minute more. Add the chopped tomatoes, (bell) pepper, tomato purée, sugar, ketchup and Worcestershire sauce to the pan, stir to combine and bring to the boil. Reduce the heat to a gentle simmer and leave to cook for 1 hour. Season to taste and keep warm.

Heat the hot dogs in simmering water or cook under a preheated grill (broiler). Place one hot dog in each bun, spoon over some of the meat mixture and top with the shallots. Serve with skin-on fries (see page 88) and onion rings (see page 93).

CHILLI CHEESE DOG

These are messy as anything to eat but seriously tasty. If you want to add an authentic Californian touch to the dog, serve with the addition of a squeeze of yellow mustard (see page 71) and some diced raw onion, just like they do at the legendary Hollywood restaurant Pink's (see 10 Famous Hot Dog Restaurants on pages 56–57). What the heck, double the recipe and have two each – you won't regret it.

Makes 4 (ORDER UP! PAGE 15)

200g/7oz chilli con carne (see page 89), warm
200ml/7fl oz/scant 1 cup cheese sauce (see page 94), warm
4 all-beef hot dogs
4 hot dog rolls, sliced top down
2 tbsp pickled chillies, sliced

Preheat the grill (broiler) to medium.

Place the hot dogs on a grill pan and place under the grill until cooked through. Place one hot dog in each roll, spoon over some of the chilli con carne and top with some of the cheese sauce. Place the hot dogs under the grill once more until the cheese sauce bubbles and begins to brown. Scatter over some of the pickled chillies and serve immediately.

WHAT'S IN YOUR HOT DOG?

The old cliché goes that if you really knew what went into a hot dog, you wouldn't want to eat one. But that's just another urban myth to file along with alligators in the sewers, at least according to America's National Hot Dog and Sausage Council. They were so fed up with the lore of lips (see Hot Dogs on Screen, page 35) that they even produced a video showing the hot dog manufacturing process.

To make a hot dog, you first start with beef, pork or chicken meat trimmed from the prime cuts, with no more than 30 per cent fat content. Offal (or 'variety meats' as they're called in America) is rarely used for hot dogs and if it is, it will be clearly stated on the packaging. However, in some instances the meat may be 'mechanically separated' and labelled as such, which involves forcing bones already trimmed of most of their meat (which has been used for other purposes) under high pressure through a sieve to separate the bone from any remaining meat tissue.

The meat is ground, then blended with seasonings and a curing agent such as sodium nitrate. Ice is also added at this point to prevent the mixture from heating up due to friction from blending, which could cause it to spoil (that does mean that your sausage will be up to 10 per cent water, however).

The now batter-like purée is poured into casings. These can be natural and made from animal intestines or collagen that's extracted from animal hides, processed into a 'dough' and then extruded. They may also be made from inedible cellulose that will be removed at the end of the process to make skinless sausages. Most hot dog connoisseurs will always go for a natural casing as it provides the distinctive 'snap' that many see as indicative of a really good dog.

The casings are pinched into 12cm (5in) or 30cm (12in) links and then hot-smoked until fully cooked. After rinsing, the hot dogs are fed through a mechanical peeler that removes the inedible casing (if used). They are then weighed, quality-checked for any breakages and packaged, usually in packs of 10, even though hot dog buns come in packs of 4, 6 or 8.

CORN DOG

It's tempting to say 'only in America' about these battered and deep-fried hot dogs on a stick, until you recall that battered sausages are a great British chip shop tradition too. The corn is used to make the thick batter that surrounds the hot dogs in the form of cornmeal, and in this recipe, kernels of sweetcorn are added to the coating for extra flavour and texture. These dogs are not served in buns but on the stick, and are perfect for dipping into sauces.

Serves 6

150g/5½oz/1 cup yellow cornmeal
100g/3½oz/1 cup plain flour
2 tsp sea salt
1 tsp baking powder
¼ tsp bicarbonate of soda (baking soda)
1 tsp paprika
1 tsp garlic powder
1 tsp onion powder
250g/9oz/scant 2½ cups sweetcorn, coarsely chopped in a food processor
1 pinch of cayenne pepper
12 beef hot dogs
350ml/12fl oz/1½ cups buttermilk
a few drops of Tabasco sauce
150g/5½oz/scant 1½ cups cornflour, for coating
3l/5¼ pints/13¼ cups vegetable oil, or enough to fill a countertop deep-fat fryer or a large heavy-based pan two-thirds full
12 wooden skewers

Combine the cornmeal, flour, salt, baking powder, bicarbonate of soda (baking soda), paprika, garlic powder and onion powder. Make a well in the centre and set aside. In a separate bowl, combine the processed sweetcorn, buttermilk and tabasco. Pour the wet ingredients into the dry ingredients and stir to combine, being careful not to overwork the batter. Set aside for 15 minutes until thickened.

Meanwhile, heat the oil in a deep-fat fryer or large pan to 180°C/350°F and thread the hot dogs lengthways onto the skewers. One at a time, coat the hot dogs in the cornflour, tapping off the excess, then dip into the corn batter to coat. Deep-fry the corn dogs for 3 minutes until golden brown, then transfer to kitchen paper to drain any excess oil.

Serve the corndogs warm with your choice of maple mustard sauce (see page 75), garlic or herb mayonnaise (see page 73), ketchup (see page 70) for dipping and a side of hot dog mac 'n' cheese (see page 94).

PO' BOY

The Po'boy is one of the American state of Louisiana's greatest culinary gifts to the world. Named after the depression-era striking New Orleans streetcar drivers it was created to feed, it can be made with roast beef and gravy, but this is an adaptation of the seafood variety which, when paired with a hot dog, makes for a very special kind of surf 'n' turf.

Serves 4

For the oysters
16 oysters, shucked, or 16 large prawns (shrimp), heads removed, shelled and de-veined
plain (all-purpose) flour for dusting, seasoned with sea salt and pepper
1 quantity beer batter (see page 93)
3l/5¼ pints/13¼ cups vegetable oil (or enough to fill a deep-fat fryer or large pan two-thirds full)
sea salt

To serve
4 hot dogs
¼ romaine or little gem lettuce, finely sliced
2 tomatoes, halved and sliced
cucumber pickles (see page 83)
4 hot dog buns

For the Creole mustard
100g/3½oz grain mustard
½ tsp celery salt
½ tsp allspice
1 tsp garlic powder
1 clove, ground in a pestle and mortar
½ teaspoon grated nutmeg

For the spicy Cajun mayo
200ml/7fl oz/scant 1 cup mayonnaise (see page 72)
2 tbsp Creole mustard (see above)
1 tsp cucumber pickle liquor
1 tsp horseradish sauce
a pinch of cayenne pepper
1 tsp paprika
1 tsp onion powder
5 drops of Tabasco sauce, or to taste
sea salt and black pepper

To make the Creole mustard and spicy Cajun mayo, combine the ingredients for each one in separate bowls, stir well and set aside. Next, heat the oil to 180°C/350°F. Pat the oysters or prawns (shrimp) dry, then toss in the seasoned flour. Dip into the batter to coat, then fry for 2–3 minutes, or until the batter is golden brown. Drain on kitchen paper, season with salt and keep warm. Grill the hot dogs in a grill pan or under an overhead grill (broiler) for 3 minutes or until cooked through. Place some of the lettuce, a few slices of tomato, the cucumber pickle and a hot dog in each bun. Tuck in three of the oysters or prawns beside the hot dog and spoon over the spicy mayonnaise.

THE RISE OF THE 'HAUTE DOG'

In the race to make every foodstuff on the planet 'artisan', it was inevitable that hot dogs would get the gourmet treatment. That generic soft white bun? It's now made from buttery brioche. Mass-produced frankfurter? Not on my watch – 100 per cent organic, fully traceable beef only, please. And let's replace onions, mustard and ketchup with, well, just about anything.

Whereas some food trends can be insufferably elitist and suck all the fun out of eating, the great thing about the haute dog trend is that it's impossible to remove hot dogs too far from their natural place on the dining scale. Because there is something inherently funny about hot dogs, and because they are so ingrained as a quick snack on the street after a night out at the cinema or a sporting event, to try and elevate them to a serious dining experience would be laughable.

It's difficult to say exactly when dogs started to go gourmet, but a notable early example is Hot Doug's in Chicago. Opened in 2001 and sadly now closed, customers queued out the door of the brightly decorated, simple diner for the foie gras and Sauternes duck sausage with truffle aïoli (garlic mayo), foie gras mousse and fleur de sel.

It wasn't long before top chefs were getting in on the gourmet hot dog act. In 2009, New York-based French-born superstar chef Daniel Boulud starting serving a range of dogs at the smart/casual DBGB in the Bowery that now includes a Thai dog with green papaya slaw, sriracha, peanuts and coriander (cilantro). At the Upper West Side's Fatty Crab, Asian fusion specialist Zak Pelaccio served up his Fatty Dog with a ground pork, shrimp, and XO sausage in a potato bread roll topped with spicy Asian aioli.

In the same year in London, Philip Howard served game consommé and bacon cream with a 'small game hot dog' made with venison, hare and pork and topped with a sweet and sour 'brown sauce' made with onions, spices, malt vinegar and beer at his Michelin-starred Kitchen W8 restaurant.

Although London's Gourmet Hot Dog Company didn't last long (closing soon after launching in 2008 due to a combination of being before its time and using poor-quality ingredients) other operators have had far more success. Bubbledogs in Fitzrovia (see page 57) has had queues out the door since launching in 2012 for its innovative combination of champagne and gourmet dogs. And you know something's gone mainstream when Jamie Oliver arrives on the scene: Jamie's Diner in London's West End offers smoked beef or free-range pork dogs on brioche buns topped with everything from hummus to pulled pork.

WORLD'S WEIRDEST HOT DOGS

In many ways, hot dogs are a blank canvas of meat and bread just waiting for a culinary artist to express their myriad gastronomic notions upon them. Or for a drunk person to empty the fridge all over them, which might just be the case with some of the following creations.

Puka Dogs

To paraphrase L. P. Hartley, Hawaii is a foreign country; they do things differently there. Why slice a hot dog roll when you can impale it on a heated rod, creating a toasted tunnel which you can slip your Polish sausage into? Just add spicy garlic lemon 'secret' sauce and fruit salsa and you're good to go. They got the name nearly right, didn't they?

Scramble Dog

The properly old-fashioned Dinglewood Pharmacy in Columbus, Georgia is the place to head if you want the genuine American soda fountain experience like you've seen in the movies and your hot dog sans bun, cut up, drowned in chilli con carne and topped with pickles, onions and crushed-up salted 'oyster' crackers. Who wouldn't?

Reindeer Dog

This Alaskan speciality is like any other hot dog, except it's made with one of Santa's sleigh-pulling team. That's OK, isn't it?

Octo Dog

There's something fishy about American celeb chef Tom Colicchio's take on a hot dog that he served at Riverpark, a smart riverside restaurant in New York. The frankfurter was replaced by a braised, smoked and grilled octopus tentacle and then topped with spicy mayo and cucumber relish.

Lobster 'Haute' Dog

As served at the Chebeague Island Inn in Maine, this is an upper-class dog made with lobster and beef, topped with avocado and garlic whip and pickled watermelon slaw.

French-fry Wrapped Dog

I think we're all going to have to move to Seoul in South Korea as they are obviously culinary geniuses. That's where you'll find this dog on a stick, coated in batter then dipped in French fries and deep-fried.

Yakisoba

You'll probably know that yakisoba is a dish of stir-fried Japanese noodles. So you'll also realize that no one – and I mean no one – would slop some yakisoba on top of a hot dog, right? Except at Japadog in Vancouver, where they also put seaweed on some of their offerings. The Canadians really do hate America, don't they?

KOREAN KIMCHI DOG

DANISH DOG

MEXICAN HOT DOG WRAP

KOREAN KIMCHI DOG

Kimchi might sound like an odd thing to put on a hot dog, but as a Korean fermented cabbage product, it's the spicy Asian cousin of the staple dog topping, sauerkraut. Made the traditional way, kimchi takes a few weeks to ferment before it's ready to eat, way too long to wait for a hot dog! So here's a quick method that retains the signature ingredients and flavours. Just don't go round telling your Korean chums it's 'authentic'. Gochugaru (Korean chilli flakes), salted shrimps and gochujang (Korean hot pepper paste) are all available online or in specialist Asian grocers.

Makes 4 (ORDER UP! PAGE 28)

100g/3½oz/scant ½ cup sea salt
50g/2oz/scant ⅓ cup caster sugar
1kg/2lb 4oz Chinese cabbage, cored and cut into 5cm/2in square pieces
6 cloves garlic, minced to a fine paste
1 thumb-sized piece of ginger, peeled and finely grated
4 tbsp fish sauce
4 tbsp soy sauce
4 tbsp gochugaru or mild chilli powder
2 tsp salted shrimp or 2 tbsp anchovy sauce

1 bunch of spring onions (scallions), finely sliced on an angle
1 carrot, sliced into julienne
1–2 tbsp gochujang (or hot sauce of your choice) depending on how hot you like your food
200ml/7fl oz/scant 1 cup mayonnaise
squeeze of lemon juice
4 pork hot dogs
4 hot dog buns, split from the top
2 tbsp sesame seeds, toasted

To make the kimchi, place 1 litre/1¾ pints/2½ cups water in a pan with the salt and sugar and bring to the boil. Stir until the salt and sugar dissolve, remove from the heat and allow to cool for 5 minutes. Put the cabbage in a bowl and pour over the cooled brine. Let stand for 30 minutes, then drain and refresh the cabbage in cold water and drain again. Combine the garlic, ginger, fish and soy sauces, gochugaru and shrimp in a bowl. Add the spring onions (scallions) and carrot and stir. Add the cabbage and stir until it is evenly coated with the spiced paste. Set aside. In a bowl, stir the gochujang into the mayonnaise and season with lemon juice to taste. Decant into a squeezy sauce bottle. Heat the hot dogs through in simmering water for 3 minutes, or according to the packet instructions. Place a hot dog sausage in each bun, top with some kimchi and squeeze over the mayonnaise sauce. Sprinkle some sesame seeds over each dog. Serve with Asian slaw (see page 81).

SPANISH DOG

This is the ideal dog to cook on the barbecue. You can cook the pepper, tomato, garlic, chorizo and hot dogs over the coals, plus the classic Catalan spicy, smoky sauce romesco will make anything else you cook on the day taste amazing. The sauce recipe calls for a whole head of garlic, but use as many or as few of the roasted cloves as you like. If it's not barbecue weather, this dog is just as easy to prepare in the kitchen.

Makes 4 (ORDER UP! PAGE 28)

3 large (bell) red peppers
250g/9oz tomatoes
1 whole bulb of garlic
2 tbsp olive oil
1 tbsp smoked paprika
25g/1oz/2 tbsp blanched almonds, toasted
25g/1oz/2 tbsp hazelnuts, skinned and toasted

1 slice of white bread, fried in olive oil until golden
1 tbsp good-quality red wine vinegar, preferably Rioja
4 small cooking chorizo sausages
sea salt and black pepper

4 pork hot dogs
4 hot dog buns

Preheat the oven to 220°C/425°F/gas mark 7. In a large bowl, toss the (bell) peppers, tomatoes and garlic in 2 tablespoons of the oil, salt and pepper. Place all the ingredients on a baking sheet and put in the oven. Cook until the skin of the tomatoes and peppers goes black and blisters and the garlic is tender (allow roughly 10 minutes for the tomatoes and 30 minutes for the peppers and garlic). Leave the cooked peppers to cool for 10–15 minutes, then skin and deseed. Set one pepper aside for the hot dogs and place the other in a food processor or blender. Skin the tomatoes and squeeze some of the cooked garlic cloves and add to the processor along with the nuts, bread, vinegar and paprika. Blitz to a coarse paste, adjust the seasoning with salt and pepper. Grill the chorizo sausages on a ridged grill pan over a high heat until nearly cooked through, for 10–15 minutes depending on size. Grill the hot dog sausages until heated through. Split the hot dog buns from the top down to just over halfway. Slice the chorizo sausage lengthways and slice the reserved pepper into quarters. Put the peppers, hot dog sausages and chorizo in the buns and top with some of the romesco sauce.

MALAYSIAN SATAY DOG

This dog brings together two great street-food traditions. Just as no visit to New York would be complete without a stop-off at a hot dog cart, you can't go to Malaysia and not get satay from a roadside or food market hawker stall. The sticks of thinly sliced marinated meat are cooked over an open fire and served with spicy peanut sauce, onion, cucumber and cubes of sticky rice. If you want to be really authentic, replace the peanut butter with finely ground unsalted roasted peanuts.

Makes 4 (ORDER UP! PAGE 29)

1 tsp dried chilli flakes
1 red onion, finely chopped
3 cloves garlic, crushed
thumb-sized piece of galangal or ginger, peeled and grated
1 lemongrass stalk, chopped
½ tsp ground cinnamon
1 tsp ground coriander
1 tsp ground cumin
1 tsp ground turmeric
1 tbsp vegetable oil
juice of 2 limes

1 tsp tamarind paste
1 tbsp sugar
150g/5½oz/generous ½ cup crunchy peanut butter
100ml/3½fl oz/scant ½ cup thick coconut milk
2 tsp sea salt
4 chicken hot dogs
1 cucumber, peeled, deseeded and finely diced.
1 red onion finely diced
4 hot dog buns

In a large pestle and mortar, make a paste from the chilli, onion, garlic, galangal (or ginger) and lemongrass, then pound in the cinnamon, coriander, cumin and turmeric. Heat the oil in a pan and fry the paste for 5 minutes until fragrant. Add a teaspoon of the lime juice, the tamarind paste and a teaspoon of the sugar and cook for a few minutes, stirring continuously. Add the peanut butter and coconut milk, bring to the boil, then reduce the heat and simmer until the oil splits. Add the salt and more of the lime juice and sugar to taste.

Cook the hot dogs on a barbecue, in a grill pan, under an overhead grill (broiler) or in simmering water. Combine the onion and cucumber in a bowl and dress with the remaining lime juice and salt to taste. Put a hot dog in each bun, spoon over some of the sauce then sprinkle over the onion and cucumber relish.

MEXICAN HOT DOG WRAP

This recipe is all sorts of culinary sacrilege so concentrate on the fact that it's delicious and ignore the food snobs. If you want a touch of authenticity to salve your gastronomic guilty conscience, then order some Mexican masa harina, a flour made from lime-soaked and cooked corn kernels, available online. If you get the Mexican bug, it's worth investing in a tortilla press, which takes all the work out of the process, but a rolling pin will do the job just as well. The recipe makes more tortillas than you need so freeze them for the next time you fancy Mexican food. Skin-on fries (see page 88) are a great side option.

Makes 4 (ORDER UP! PAGE 29)

For the guacamole
2 ripe avocados, peeled and stoned
1 green chilli, chopped
½ bunch of coriander (cilantro), chopped
juice of 1 lime
sea salt

For the tortillas
500g/1lb 2oz/4 cups masa harina, fine cornmeal or plain (all-purpose) flour
50ml/2fl oz/scant ¼ cup olive oil, plus extra for frying
350 ml/12 fl oz/1½ cups tepid water

For the salsa
4 tomatoes, peeled, deseeded and roughly chopped
1 red onion, roughly chopped
1 jalapeño chilli, deseeded and finely chopped
5 drops of Tabasco sauce
½ bunch of coriander (cilantro), chopped
juice of 1 lime

To serve
8 pork hot dogs
4 tbsp sour cream

Purée the guacamole ingredients and chill until required. For the tortillas, combine the flour and 1 tsp salt in a bowl and pour in the oil. Add 300ml/10fl oz/1¼ cups of water and mix until you achieve a soft dough, adding extra water if needed. Knead on a floured surface for 5 minutes, then return to the bowl and leave to rest under a damp cloth for 10 minutes. Meanwhile, combine the salsa ingredients in a bowl. Cover with cling film and set aside. Divide the dough into 12 pieces, shape into balls then roll into 5mm/¼in-thick discs. In a frying pan over a medium heat, cook the tortillas for 1 minute per side, or until brown spots start to appear. Keep warm in the oven while you cook the other tortillas. Heat the hot dogs according to the packet instructions. Spread guacamole over each tortilla and top with 2 hot dogs, some salsa and 1 tbsp of sour cream. Wrap the tortilla around the filling and enjoy.

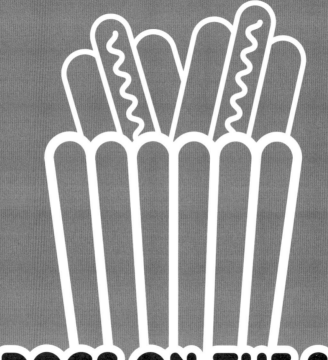

HOT DOGS ON THE SCREEN

Hot dogs have appeared in so many film and TV shows that they ought to have their own agent. Here's a selection of five favourite moments. Warning: due to high levels of hilarity, watching while consuming a hot dog may constitute a choking hazard.

The Muppets TV Show: The Swedish chef cooks hot dogs (1976)
The famously incomprehensible cook (played by Muppet creators Jim Henson and Frank Oz themselves) tosses a hot dog into a steaming pan of water. Miss Piggy arrives looking for her pet dog, Foo Foo (this was a more innocent time, or was it?). The chef informs her that 'the dog is in the potty'. Enraged, she throws a karate chop which the chef deflects with a saucepan lid. The skit ends with the chef showing a surprised and relieved Miss Piggy the now cooked sausage.

Sudden Impact (1983)
Best known for his 'Go ahead, make my day' catchphrase, Clint Eastwood's seminal cop character, Inspector 'Dirty' Harry Callahan, also proves to be something of a gourmet. In a break from hunting down a revenge killer, Callahan takes the time to tell a fellow detective, 'Having to wade through the scum of this city, being swept away by bigger and bigger waves of corruption, apathy and red tape. Nah, that doesn't bother me. But you know what does bother me? Watching you stuff your face with those hot dogs. Nobody, I mean nobody, puts ketchup on a hot dog.'

The Great Outdoors (1988)
This slight comedy about a summer family vacation in Wisconsin gone wrong boasts two legends of American comedy: Dan Ackroyd and the late John Candy. Ackroyd's character, Roman Craig, a full-of-himself investment banker, is barbecuing lobsters for Chicagoan nice guy Chet Ripley and both of their wives. Pointing at Ripley, Craig announces 'How about the gourmet here, you know what he wanted? Hot dogs! You know what they make those things out of, Chet? You know? Lips and a**holes!'

Seinfeld: Season 9, Episode 8 (1997)
This episode of stand-up comedian Jerry Seinfeld's hugely popular show is memorable because it must be the only sitcom to be inspired by the reverse chronological structure of Harold Pinter's 1978 play *Betrayal*. In one of several interweaved plotlines, Seinfeld's neighbour, Kramer, discovers that hot dog vendor Franklin Delano Romanowski (FDR) has wished for Kramer to drop dead and will only recant if Kramer takes a snowball to the head. FDR's vendetta is explained at the end of the episode, when a flashback to two years earlier shows Kramer throwing a snowball at him.

30 Rock: Season 1, Episode 1 (2006)
In Tina Fey's brilliant sitcom, TV producer Liz Lemon (played by Fey) is queuing for a hot dog outside the studios at 30 Rockefeller Plaza in New York when somebody decides to form his own line on the other side of the cart, effectively jumping the whole queue. When some of the original queue defects to the interloper's side, Lemon announces 'I want all the hot dogs. And I'm giving them to the good people' pointing at the remaining queue behind her. Yay, Liz Lemon!

HOT DOG SONGS

Hot dogs have been featured in popular music for almost as long as sausages have been put in buns (see Lil Johnson's risqué 'Sam, The Hot Dog Man' from the 1930s) and often in surprising ways. Here's the ideal soundtrack to any hot dog cooking and eating marathon.

Hot Dog, Buddy, Buddy
Bill Haley and the Comets (1956)
In no way a total cash-in retread of the kiss-curled bopper's greatest hit 'Rock Around the Clock' from the year before. Well, actually it is, just with some bizarre, cobbled-together lyrics referencing everyone's favourite finger food, such as: 'Cause I'm rocking, rocking on down the line, hot dog buddy buddy, a hot dog all the time'. It does, however, whip along at a decent pace, driven by that instantly recognisable echoing, snapping snare drum.

Tropical Hot Dog Night
Captain Beefheart (1978)
If you've never listened to the avant-garde blues/rock stylings of the late, great Don Van Vliet (dubbed Captain Beefheart by his friend and fellow freak, Frank Zappa), then this slice of mutant calypso is a great place to start. A lilting beat, churning guitars, an ear worm of a melodic brass riff and the Captain growling about 'two flamingos in a fruit fight'. Hot dog heaven.

Hot Dog
Led Zeppelin (1979)
A deep cut from the heavy rock behemoth's least-loved final album *In Through the Out Door*, this is the hairy foursome in full-on supercharged rockabilly mode, complete with naff Presley-isms from singer Robert Plant who intones 'Aaahh, hot dog' as Jimmy Page pulls out all his best Scotty Moore (Elvis's original guitar player) licks.

King of Rock 'n' Roll
Prefab Sprout (1988)
Altogether now: 'Hot dog, jumping frog, Albuquerque'. Prefab Sprout frontman Paddy McAloon may have the voice of an angel and the lyric-writing ability to match, but he was in playful, throwaway mood on the band's biggest hit. The must-see video features the band lounging poolside while statues sing, a frog waiter delivers cocktails and a trio of hot dogs dance for McAloon and chums' entertainment.

Hot Dog
LMFAO (2011)
Over a Sylvester-style 70's disco beat, the self-proclaimed 'dog-alcoholic' LA rap duo (made up of the son and grandson of Motown record label boss Berry Gordy Jr) defend their right to eat a hot dog after burning calories on the dance floor, only to be disappointed by the vendor's lack of onions, peppers and bacon-wrapped dogs. Oh, the humanity!

INDIAN CHAPATI HOT DOG WRAP

MIDDLE EASTERN HOT DOG

THAI DOG

You'll need to pay your local Asian grocer a visit for some of the ingredients in this curry paste but the results are well worth the effort, though you could use a pre-made version at a pinch. This will make more sauce than you need, so either invite friends round and serve a whole lot more hot dogs or freeze the remainder for when you next feel the need for some exotic spice in your life.

Serves 4 (ORDER UP! PAGE 39)

3 green bird's eye chillies
sea salt
1 tbsp chopped galangal
2 tbsp chopped lemongrass
1 tbsp chopped kaffir lime zest
1 tbsp chopped coriander (cilantro)
2 tbsp chopped shallots
2 tbsp chopped garlic
1 tsp Thai shrimp paste

150ml/5½fl oz/ ⅔ cup coconut cream
1 tbsp palm sugar (jiggery)
1 tbsp fish sauce
400ml/14fl oz can light coconut milk
12 leaves Thai holy basil, torn
4 chicken hot dogs
4 hot dog buns, split from the top
4 tbsp crispy shallots (see page 79)
4 long red Thai chillies, sliced

In a large pestle and mortar, grind the chillies to a paste; a pinch of sea salt will help the process. Add the galangal, lemongrass, lime zest, coriander (cilantro), shallots, garlic and shrimp paste and continue to grind to a smooth paste. Alternatively, put all the ingredients in a blender with a teaspoon of water for 3–4 minutes.

In a large wok, bring the coconut cream to the boil. When the oil begins to separate, add 2–3 tbsp of your paste (depending on how hot you want your curry) and stir fry for a few minutes until it releases its aromas. Add the sugar and fish sauce and stir well. Pour in the coconut milk and bring to a simmer. Cook for 30 minutes, or until the mixture has thickened enough to coat the back of a spoon. Stir in the basil and keep warm.

Heat the hot dogs through in simmering water for 3 minutes, or according to the manufacturer's instructions. Place one dog in each bun, top with some of the sauce and sprinkle over the shallots and chillies. Serve with Asian slaw (see page 81).

INDIAN CHAPATI HOT DOG WRAP

This recipe is really handy to have in your back pocket. Not only is it an unusual and spicy twist on a hot dog, but the sauce can be used as the base for a more traditional Indian meal. Just add about 700g/1lb 9oz of meat or fish to the curry (enough for 4 people) and serve with the chapatis and raita. Grind the fennel, cumin and coriander seeds for the curry sauce in a pestle and mortar to release their flavour. Keep the curry sauce and chaptis warm until you're ready to eat. Serve these dogs with skin-on fries (see page 88) or potato salad (see page 91) and some extra raita.

Serves 8 (ORDER UP! PAGE 38)

For the chapati
180g/6oz/scant 1½ cups chapati flour
4 tbsp ghee or butter, melted

For the curry sauce
1 tbsp vegetable oil
1 onion, finely chopped
2 cloves garlic, finely chopped
1 tbsp garam masala
1 tsp each of fennel seeds, cumin seeds and coriander seeds, ground
1 tsp chilli powder
400g/14oz tin chopped tomatoes
sea salt and black pepper

For the raita
250g/9oz/1 cup natural Greek yogurt
1 small cucumber, deseeded and finely chopped
1 green chilli, deseeded and finely chopped
1 tsp ground cumin
½ tsp mild chilli powder
1 tbsp chopped coriander (cilantro)
juice of 1 lemon, to season

To serve
8 hot dogs
200g/7oz caramelized onions (page 78)

Put the flour in a bowl and gradually add 150ml/¼ pint/scant ¾ cup water, kneading as you go until you have a soft, elastic dough. Cover and leave to rest. For the sauce, heat the oil in a pan over a medium heat and cook the onion until soft. Add the garlic and cook for 1 minute, then add the garam masala, ground seeds and chilli powder and cook for 2 minutes. Stir in the tomatoes, bring to the boil, then simmer for 30 minutes until thick. Season. Combine the raita ingredients and season with lemon juice and salt to taste. Divide the dough into 8 balls, then roll out on a floured surface to 15cm/6in rounds. Cook in a dry pan over a medium heat for 1 minute per side, then brush with ghee. Grill (broil) the hot dogs until cooked. Spoon some sauce onto each chapati. Top with a hot dog, onions and raita, then roll up and serve.

MIDDLE EASTERN HOT DOG

This recipe brings all the classic flavours of the Middle East into one wrap. Za'tar is a traditional spice mix typically made from thyme, oregano, marjoram, sesame seeds, sumac and salt and adds a wonderfully aromatic note to the bread. This recipe will make more flatbreads than you need but the remainder will freeze successfully.

Serves 8 (ORDER UP! PAGE 39)

For the flatbreads
500g/1lb 2oz/4 cups strong white
   bread flour, plus extra for dusting
1 tbsp olive oil
1 tbsp za'tar
1 tsp sea salt

For the harissa paste
2 roast red (bell) peppers
6 cloves garlic, crushed
2–4 red chillies, deseeded and chopped
10 mint leaves
1 tsp each of cumin seeds and
   coriander seeds, toasted for
   1 minute in a dry pan, ground
2–3 tbsp olive oil

For the harissa mayo
1 tbsp harissa paste
200ml/7fl oz/scant 1 cup mayonnaise
   (see page 72)

For the hummus
400g/14oz tin chickpeas, drained
175g/6oz tahini
1 clove garlic, minced to a fine paste
juice of 1 lemon, to season

To serve
8 hot dogs
1 small bunch of parsley, leaves
   picked
1 small bunch of coriander (cilantro),
   chopped
1 red onion, finely sliced
1 lemon, halved

Make the flatbread dough by putting the flour into the bowl of a stand mixer. Combine the oil and za'tar and add to the bowl. Add the salt, then, using the dough hook attachment on a slow speed, mix the flour, salt and oil mixture, then add 300ml/½ pint/1¼ cups of tepid water until a smooth dough is formed. Add more water if the dough doesn't come together or looks dry. Alternatively, work the dough together in a large mixing bowl by hand and knead on a lightly floured surface until smooth. Cover and rest while you make the other elements.

To make the harissa paste, combine the peppers, garlic, chillies, mint, cumin and coriander in a mini food processor. Add a tablespoon of the oil and process until smooth, adding more of the oil if the paste fails to come together or is too dry. To make the harissa mayonnaise, stir the paste into the mayonnaise and set aside.

Make the hummus by blending the chickpeas, tahini and garlic in a food processor until smooth. Season with the salt and lemon juice to taste and set aside.

Divide the dough into 12 pieces and roll into balls. Flatten each ball into a 5mm/¼in-thick disc. Put a pan, large enough to accommodate the flatbreads, over a medium heat. Fry the breads for one minute per side, or until brown spots start to appear. Keep warm in the oven while you finish cooking the remaining flatbreads.

To serve, cook the hot dogs on a barbecue, in a grill pan, under an overhead grill (broiler) or in simmering water for 3 minutes, or until heated through. Spread the flatbreads with some of the hummus and place a hot dog in the centre. Top with some of the parsley, coriander (cilantro) and red onion, squeeze over some of the harissa mayonnaise, and finish with a squeeze of lemon juice. Wrap the bread around the filling and serve with skin-on fries (see page 88) or potato salad (see page 91) and onion rings (see page 93).

SUNDAY ROAST DOG

I know it sounds insane, but trust me, this is a truly delicious dog. It's best made using up leftovers from your Sunday lunch, but it's worth making from scratch too. If you want to cheat, you could use packet bread sauce mix, packet stuffing with some added fresh herbs and sautéed onions, and gravy just made with chicken stock and gravy powder. If you can't find sausage meat, use one pack of pork sausages removed from their skins. Serve with poutine (see page 95).

Serves 4 (ORDER UP! PAGE 38)

For the bread sauce
500ml/18fl oz/2 cups whole milk
3 black peppercorns
1 tsp cloves
1 bay leaf
2 shallots, sliced
150g/5½oz/scant 1½ cups fresh white breadcrumbs
large knob of butter
sea salt and black pepper

To serve
4 brioche hot dog buns, sliced
4 chicken hot dogs
4 tbsp caramelized onions (see page 78)

For the gravy
50g/2oz butter
50g/2oz/½ cup plain (all-purpose) flour
250ml/9fl oz/generous 1 cup white wine
500ml/18fl oz/2 cups chicken stock
1 tbsp gravy powder (optional)

For the stuffing
1 tbsp vegetable oil
1 onion, finely chopped
400g/14oz sausage meat
12 sage leaves, chopped
150g/5½oz/scant 1½ cups fresh white breadcrumbs
1 egg, beaten

For the bread sauce, combine the milk, peppercorns, cloves, bay leaf and shallots in a pan. Bring to the boil, then remove from the heat, cover and leave to infuse for 2 hours. Strain the milk into a clean pan over a gentle heat. Whisk in the breadcrumbs and stir until the mixture thickens. Whisk in the butter, season to taste and set aside.

For the stuffing, preheat your oven to 180°C/350°F/gas mark 4 and lightly oil a baking sheet. Heat the oil in a heavy-based pan over a medium heat and fry the onion for 7–10 minutes until soft and translucent. Put in a bowl with the remaining stuffing ingredients, season and mix well. Form the mixture into 12 balls, transfer to the oiled baking sheet and cook for 25 minutes. For the gravy, knead together the butter and flour in a bowl. Place the white wine in a saucepan and reduce to a syrup (you'll be left with about 1 tbsp of liquid at the most), add the chicken stock and reduce by a third. Whisk in the butter and flour mixture until you have a thick gravy. Cook the hot dogs according to the packet instructions. Spread some bread sauce inside each bun. Thinly slice the stuffing balls and place 4 or 5 slices in each bun. Top with a hot dog, onions and a little of the gravy and serve.

If there's an intrinsically funny food, it's the hot dog. Silly name and suggestive shape aside, hot dogs are associated with fun times – a ball game, a barbecue or a snack on a boozy night out. So here are a few jokes to add extra relish to those occasions.

A man walks into a doctor's office with hot dogs in his ears and nose and says, 'Doctor, I feel terrible. I'm having difficulty breathing and even worse, I think I'm going deaf.' The doctor replies, 'Relax, you just need to start eating more sensibly.'

Q: How do you make a hot dog stand?
A: Steal its chair.

A Buddhist walks up to a hot dog vendor in New York and says, 'Make me one with everything.' The vendor, who's heard that one before, smiles to himself and makes the dog with onions, mustard, ketchup and sauerkraut, as requested. The Buddhist pays with a $5 bill and asks for change. The vendor looks solemnly at the Buddhist, taps his chest and says, 'Change comes from within.'

Q: Why did the female hot dog seller get the sack?
A: She kept putting her hair in a bun.

A hot dog received a letter from the *Reader's Digest*. It read, 'You may already be a wiener.'

A man goes to the vet because his dog is running a high temperature. The vet takes one look at the panting animal and says, 'Please wait, I'll be right back.' Within moments he returns holding a bottle of French's. The man, looking puzzled asks, 'I thought you'd prescribe some pills, what on earth are you going to do with that?' The vet replies, 'Everyone knows mustard is the best thing for a hot dog.'

Q: What did the New York hot dog say to the Chicago hot dog?
A: 'We'll ketchup with you eventually'.

Q: Why did the shy hot dog seller quit his job?
A: He didn't like it when the customers checked out his buns.

A parched hot dog walks into a bar and orders a beer. The barman looks the hot dog up and down and then shakes his head. The hot dog, now furious as well as thirsty, demands to know why he can't get a drink. 'Sorry,' says the barman. 'We don't serve food here.'

Q: Why did the allium farmer make a particularly good hot dog salesman?
A: He really knew his onions.

A young hot dog asks his mother, 'Where do I come from?' The mother replies, 'Son, you really don't want to know.'

Q: What did the hot dog sausage call his private detective agency?
A: Frank Furtive.

Customer: You've put the wrong condiment on my hot dog!
Vendor: I'm sorry, there mustard been some misunderstanding.

HOT DOG QUIZ

Grill your chums on their hot dog knowledge with our telling questions. Who will end up with mustard all down their shirt and who will be the overall 'wiener'?

1. What sort of buns are Chicago hot dogs always served in?
a) pretzel
b) soft white
c) poppy seed

2. Who was the British-born entrepreneur who is credited with bringing hot dogs to American baseball stadiums?
a) Harry Stevens
b) Steven Harrison
c) Harrison Ford

3. Where is America's annual 4th July international hot dog eating championship held?
a) Wiener Circle, Chicago
b) Nathan's Famous, Coney Island
c) Nu-Way, Macon, Georgia

4. Which European city do wiener sausages originally come from?
a) Hamburg
b) Zagreb
c) Vienna

5. Which British royal famously ate a hot dog with a knife and fork?
a) Princess Diana
b) Prince Philip
c) Queen Elizabeth

6. If you are eating a bacon-wrapped dog topped with pinto beans and other items, which American state are you most likely to be in?
a) New Mexico
b) Arizona
c) Utah

7. Which cartoon character's first words on screen were 'hot dogs, hot dogs'?
a) Mickey Mouse
b) Bart Simpson
c) Peter Griffin

8. In which restaurant do the servers shout 'What'll ya have!?' as customers approach the counter?
a) Bubbledogs
b) Feltman's
c) The Varsity

9. In which German city did currywurst originate?
a) Berlin
b) Cologne
c) Munich

10. In which LA hot dog stand did *Die Hard* actor Bruce Willis reportedly propose to his now ex-wife Demi Moore?
a) Tommy's
b) Larry's
c) Pink's

11. Which New York hot dog stand is favoured by TV presenter and *Kitchen Confidential* author Anthony Bourdain?
a) Papaya King
b) Gray's Papaya
c) Shake Shack

12. Why do some hot dogs 'snap' when you bite into them?
a) due to the use of a natural casing
b) because they've been cooked on a charcoal grill
c) because they are made of all beef

1:C 2:A 3:B 4:C 5:C 6:B 7:A 8:C 9:A 10:C 11:B 12:A

BLUE CHEESE AND BACON DOG

BBQ DOG WITH PULLED PORK

BBQ DOG WITH PULLED PORK

As Frank Sinatra once memorably sang, 'hot dogs and barbecue, go together like a horse and carriage.' Actually, he didn't, because it doesn't scan and he would have sounded like an idiot, but the sentiment would have been true. This recipe makes much more pork than you'll need for the hot dogs, so make an afternoon of it and cook up some of your other barbecue favourites. Slow cooking on a barbecue is a bit of an art, so unless you really know what you're doing, it's best to cook the pork in the oven. To make a meal of the pork, serve it with some potato salad (see page 91) and coleslaw (see page 80).

Serves 8 (ORDER UP! PAGE 51)

50g/2oz smoked paprika
50g/2oz/¼ cup brown sugar
2 tsp celery salt
2 tsp onion salt
1 tsp ground cumin
1 tbsp garlic powder
1 tsp mustard powder
1.5kg/3lb 5oz bone-in pork shoulder

60g/2¼oz/¼ cup soft brown sugar
3 tbsp red wine vinegar
1 tbsp smoked paprika
½ tsp cayenne pepper

½ tsp celery salt
2 tbsp yellow mustard (see page 71)
20g/¾oz chipotle peppers in adobo sauce, chopped
250ml/9fl oz/generous 1 cup (see page 70)
2 tsp Worcestershire sauce

200g/7oz caramelized onions (see page 78)
8 beef hot dogs
8 hot dog buns

In a small bowl, mix the smoked paprika, sugar, salts, garlic and mustard powder, and cumin. Pat the meat dry with kitchen paper and then rub the spice mix over the meat (you may not need all the mix). Cover the meat and allow to rest for at least an hour in the fridge. Preheat the oven to 150°C/300°F/gas mark 2. Transfer the pork to a large roasting pan and place in the oven to cook for 4 hours. Leave to rest for 20 minutes then, using two forks, shred the meat away from the bone. Keep warm.

Meanwhile, mix the sauce ingredients in a pan, bring to the boil, then reduce to a simmer and stir for 15 minutes until thick. Set aside until cool. Grill the hot dogs in a grill pan or under an overhead grill (broiler) until heated through. Place a hot dog in each bun, top with some of the pulled pork and onions, then top with barbecue sauce.

BLUE CHEESE AND BACON DOG

Blue cheese and bacon is a combo more usually associated with burgers, but it works just as well on your favourite dog. Gorgonzola would be perfect for this recipe as it has just the right amount of salty, earthy flavour, but use whichever blue cheese you prefer.

Serves 4 (ORDER UP! PAGE 81)

8 rashers dry cure streaky bacon
200ml/7fl oz/scant 1 cup mayonnaise
(see page 72)
5 tbsp double (heavy) cream
5 tbsp buttermilk
1 clove garlic, minced to a fine paste
100g/3½oz blue cheese, mashed to
a paste
1 pinch of cayenne pepper
lemon juice, to taste
sea salt and black pepper
4 pork or beef hot dogs
4 hot dog buns, split from the top
200g/7oz caramelized onions (see
page 78)

Heat the oven to 180°C/350°F/gas mark 4.

Lay the bacon on a rack over a lipped baking tray and cook in the oven for 15 minutes, or until crisp. Drain on kitchen paper, allow to cool, then chop into bite-sized pieces.

Make the blue cheese dressing by combining the mayonnaise, cream, buttermilk, garlic, cheese, cayenne and lemon juice in a bowl and mixing well. Decant into a plastic squeezy sauce bottle.

Heat the hot dogs through in simmering water for 3 minutes, or according to the manufacturer's instructions. Place a hot dog into each bun. Top with some of the onions and scatter over some of the bacon. Squeeze over some of the blue cheese dressing. Serve with skin-on fries (see page 88) and onion rings (see page 93).

PIZZA DOG

This recipe is the equivalent of a simple cheese and tomato margherita pizza. It's delicious as it is, but you can think of it as a canvas on which to live out your pizza fantasies, adding pepperoni, strips of roasted pepper, chillies or whatever takes your fancy.

Serves 4 (ORDER UP! PAGE 50)

1 medium onion, finely chopped
1 tbsp olive oil
1 clove garlic, minced to a fine paste
400 g/14 oz tin chopped tomatoes
2 tsp dried oregano
1–4 tbsp ketchup (see page 70)
1 ball fresh mozzarella
4 tbsp grated Parmesan

4 pork or beef hot dogs
4 hot dog buns, split from the top
sea salt and black pepper

In a heavy-based pan, cook the onion in the oil over a medium heat until softened and translucent, but not coloured. Add the garlic and cook for 1 minute until its aromas are released. Add the tomatoes and oregano, season with salt and pepper and bring to the boil. Simmer very gently for 30–45 minutes. Check the flavour and add as much of the ketchup as you think necessary. The sweet sauce balances the natural acidity of the tomatoes, which will vary according to which brand of tomatoes you use.

Preheat your grill (broiler) to medium. Heat the hot dogs through in simmering water for 3 minutes, or according to the manufacturer's instructions. Place a hot dog in each bun and spoon over some of the tomato sauce. Break off small pieces of mozzarella and dot them over the sauce, then sprinkle over the Parmesan. Place under the grill for 1 minute, or until the cheese begins to bubble and brown. Allow to cool slightly before eating. Serve with skin-on fries (see page 88), potato knish (see page 92) or potato salad (see page 91) and onion rings (see page 93).

HOT DOG TRIVIA

In their more than century-long history, hot dogs have broken world records, gone to the moon and dined with royalty. Maybe they're not so trivial after all...

In 1939, a British royal visit to the upstate New York home of President Franklin D. Roosevelt saw a bamboozled Queen Elizabeth (the future Queen Mother) reach for the cutlery, despite the President's encouragement to get her hands dirty.

During the filming of the notorious hot dog eating scene in *Dumb and Dumber To*, actor Jim Carrey claims to have consumed 36 hot dogs, bitten through his tongue and inhaled a 'chunk of hot dog' into his lung.

In, 1957 the U.S. Chamber of Commerce officially named July 'National Hot Dog Month', and it's still celebrated to this day.

Although Mickey Mouse made his screen debut in *Steamboat Willie* in 1928, it wasn't until the following year's *The Karnival Kid* that he actually got to deliver his first line. And the most famous cartoon character in the world's first words? 'Hot dogs, hot dogs'.

Hot dogs helped astronaut Neil Armstrong take one giant leap for mankind, as they were part of the rations on board the 1969 Apollo 11 mission to the moon.

The world's largest hot dog to date weighed a whopping 56kg (123lb) with just under half that total coming from a sausage that took three hours to grill at the Miami-Dade County Fair and Exposition in 2014.

The longest hot dog in the world was made in Paraguay in 2011 and measured 203.80 metres (670 feet), enough to feed 2,000 people when it was portioned up.

British horticulturalist and amateur gourmet Archibald Prichard-Smyth (now recognized as a major influence on modern British food writers) was banned from the city of Chicago in 1927 when it was discovered that he'd written in his book *On Matters of the Gut* that hot dogs were 'a culinary abomination that no gentleman should let pass between his lips'.

Hot dog manufacturer Oscar Meyer's famous promotional hot dog on wheels the Wienermobile (oscarmayer.com/wienermobile) has been touring America since 1936, but has hit the headlines for the wrong reasons on more than one occasion. In 2009 it crashed into a house in Wisconsin when the driver accidentally put the 8m (27ft)-long vehicle in a forward gear while trying to reverse out of the driveway, and in 2015, the Wienermobile caused traffic chaos in central Pennsylvania when it skidded off an icy road and crashed into a telegraph pole.

10 FAMOUS HOT DOG RESTAURANTS

Whether you prefer the elegant simplicity of a New York dog or the wildly inventive wieners of a top gourmet chef, we've got the restaurant for you.

Nathan's Famous, Coney Island, New York, USA

(nathansfamous.com)
Opened in 1916 by Nathan Handwerker, this is arguably the most famous hot dog stand in the world, and home to the annual fourth of July hot dog-eating competition. Over the years, the all-beef hot dogs, made to a recipe created by Handwerker's wife Ida, have been eaten by everyone from Al Capone to Jacqueline Kennedy.

Gray's Papaya, New York, USA

(grayspapayanyc.com)
Who could argue with native New Yorker and author of *Kitchen Confidential* Anthony Bourdain's favourite hot dog spot? 'It's that particularly New York smell of hot dogs seared on kitchen foil, sauerkraut and the foamy deliciousness of a nutritious papaya drink,' says Bourdain.

The Varsity, Atlanta, USA
(thevarsity.com)
'What'll ya have!?' yell the staff from behind the counter of this drive-in diner that opened in 1928. An art deco gem, the restaurant's site covers two acres and can accommodate 600 vehicles served by carhops. Ask for a 'heavy dog' if you like plenty of chilli.

Wiener Circle, Chicago, USA
(wienercircle.net)
Chicagoans come here as much for the ferociously foul-mouthed banter from the comically hostile staff as they do for the classic Chicago-style dogs. Just make sure you know if you want a Vienna red hot (boiled) or a char dog (grilled), or be prepared to get your hair blown back by the impatient staff.

Cozy Dog, Springfield, Illinois, USA
(cozydogdrivein.com)
Opened in 1946, this unassuming family-run drive-in on Route 66 claims to be the home of the corn dog (see page 22). The Oscar Meyer dogs are threaded onto sticks, hand-dipped in the original 1940s recipe batter and fried vertically on a stick in vegetable shortening in special racks.

Coney Island Hot Dog Stand, Bailey, Colorado, USA
Want to eat hot dogs inside a 33-ton concrete replica of your favourite sausage-based finger food? Of course you do. Just head out west of Bailey and you'll find the 1950s stand by the roadside. The 42-foot long building is complete with painted-on green relish and yellow mustard.

Rutt's Hut, Clifton, New Jersey, USA
(ruttshut.com)
Home of the 'ripper' hot dog, so called because the casing is ripped open by the hot oil as it's deep fried. Originally opened in 1928 as a roadside stand and now a restaurant bar, Rutt's is equally renowned for its mustard-based relish made with cabbage, onions, carrots and a secret spice blend (it was always going to be secret, wasn't it?).

Bubbledogs, London, UK
(bubbledogs.co.uk)
Champagne and hot dogs might seem a mad mix, but sommelier Sandia Chang hit upon an enthusiastic and previously untapped audience with her clever idea to democratize artisan 'grower' champagnes by serving them alongside partner and haute cuisine chef James Knappet's gourmet hot dogs, including a Reuben dog with grilled sauerkraut, Russian dressing and Swiss cheese.

Primo's, Leeds, UK
(primosgourmethotdogs.co.uk)
This modern and recently opened restaurant in the stunning setting of the Victorian corn exchange in Leeds in Yorkshire is home to some of the most authentic hot dogs outside of the United States. As well as classic New Chicago-style dogs, the restaurant also serves the Spanish Harlem with chorizo chilli, pico salsa, Monterey Jack cheese and sour cream.

Pink's, Los Angeles, USA
(pinkshollywood.com)
Starting out as Paul and Betty Pink's pushcart in 1939, Pink's has grown into a full-blown restaurant with linen and flowers on every table and the walls covered in the headshots of its many celebrity customers, including Bruce Willis (who proposed to ex-wife Demi Moore at Pink's) and Tom Hanks. The movie-themed dogs include 'Lord of the Rings', a frankfurter threaded through onion rings (see what they did there?) in a bun topped with barbecue sauce.

KNOW YOUR BUNS

If you want to re-create an authentic ballpark or street cart hot dog experience at home, then you really need to steam your buns. Steaming not only warms the buns through, but makes them softer and more easily digestible. There are several ways to steam a hot-dog bun, all easy and none of them takes longer than a hot dog takes to cook, so make sure you have all your relishes, toppings and sides ready to go.

If you're warming your hot dogs through in simmering water, then you're already creating steam, so it's just a matter of how to capture it and put it to work. One of the least expensive options is a bamboo steamer basket that can be bought very cheaply from most kitchenware stores or Asian supermarkets. Traditionally used for cooking items like Chinese-style steamed buns and dumplings, they are perfect for hot dog buns too; just make sure the basket is deep and wide enough to hold a few buns at a time and that it's the correct diameter to fit on top of one of your pans. Simply put the buns in the basket, place the basket on top of the pan and cover with the steamer's lid. Steam for 2 minutes, then serve immediately. You can also buy metal steamer inserts for your saucepans, and some pans even come with removable steamer inserts, useful if you plan to do a lot of cooking with steam – or steam a lot of hot dog buns!

If you're grilling (broiling) your hot dogs, then simply spray your buns with water using a misting spray bottle (available in kitchenware or hardware stores) wrap them in kitchen foil and place under the grill (broiler) for 2 minutes, turning after 1 minute. Remove from the grill and allow to cool for a few seconds before unwrapping (use kitchen tongs so you don't burn yourself), and serve immediately.

You can also steam your buns in the microwave. Put the buns, still in their bag, into the microwave oven (check if the bag is secured with a metal tie and make sure you remove it before putting the bag of buns in the oven) and cook on full power for 1–2 minutes, depending on how many buns you are steaming. Carefully remove the bag and allow to rest for 30 seconds before opening, taking care to avoid any hot steam. If you only want to heat one or two buns, dampen some kitchen paper with water misting spray and wrap around the buns before microwaving on full power for 1 minute.

HOT DOG BUNS

Making your own buns makes a huge difference to the finished product, and it's one of the most rewarding ways to spend a few hours in the kitchen. It does take a little bit of time, but most of that is spent waiting for the dough to rise so you can get on with other recipes from this book in the meantime. Add the poppy seeds if you're using the buns to make Chicago-style hot dogs (see page 16).

Makes 8 (ORDER UP! PAGE 61)

200ml/7fl oz/scant 1 cup tepid milk
100ml/3½fl oz/scant ½ cup tepid water
2 tbsp caster (superfine) sugar
14 g/½ oz dried yeast
2 tsp sea salt
2 tbsp vegetable oil
500g/1lb 2oz/4 cups strong white
    bread flour, plus extra for dusting
1 egg, beaten
8 tsp poppy seeds (optional)

Preheat your oven to 220°C/425°F/gas mark 7 and grease a large baking sheet.

In the bowl of a stand mixer, dissolve the sugar in the water, then add all the other ingredients. Using the dough hook attachment on a slow speed, knead the dough until it pulls away from the side of the bowl – this will take 8–10 minutes. Alternatively, make the dough in a large mixing bowl and then knead by hand for 10 minutes on a lightly floured work surface. Cover and set aside in a warm place for about an hour until almost doubled in size.

Divide the dough into eight equal-size pieces, form into hot dog roll shapes and place on the prepared baking sheet. Allow to rise a second time until doubled in size. Put a roasting pan of water in the bottom of your oven to create some steam. Brush the rolls with the beaten egg and sprinkle on the poppy seeds, if using.

Bake for 20 minutes, or until the buns are nicely coloured. Remove to a wire rack and allow to cool.

PRETZEL HOT DOG BUNS

BRIOCHE HOT DOG BUNS

HOT DOG BUNS

BRIOCHE HOT DOG BUNS

These buns are enriched with butter and are perfect for the po'boy recipe on page 23. It is possible to make this dough by hand but it's a lot of work, so a stand mixer is highly recommended.

Makes 12 (ORDER UP! PAGE 61)

7 g/¼ oz packet dried yeast
2 tsp sea salt
125ml/4fl oz/½ cup whole milk, warm
500g/1lb 2oz/4 cups strong white
    bread flour, plus extra for dusting
3 large eggs

100g/3½oz unsalted butter, softened
1 tbsp caster (superfine) sugar
1 beaten egg, for glazing

Preheat your oven to 220°C/425°F/gas mark 7 and grease 2 large baking sheets.

In the bowl of a stand mixer, put the yeast, salt, milk, flour and eggs with 125ml/4fl oz/½ cup water. Using a dough hook, knead the mixture on a slow speed until a smooth and elastic dough is formed – this will take about 10 minutes. Alternatively, combine the ingredients in a large bowl and work the mixture with a wooden spoon for 20 minutes.

In a separate bowl, cream the butter and sugar together until smooth. With the mixer still going, add the butter mixture to the dough a little at a time, ensuring that each piece is completely amalgamated with the dough before adding the next. Cover and leave in a warm place for about 2 hours, or until doubled in size.

Divide the dough into 12 equal-sized pieces, form into hot dog roll shapes and place on the greased baking sheets. Allow to rise a second time until doubled in size. Put a roasting pan of water in the bottom of your oven to create some steam. Brush the rolls with the beaten egg and bake for 20 minutes, or until nicely coloured. Remove to a wire rack and allow to cool.

PRETZEL HOT DOG BUNS

Forget those packets of small crunchy snacks, this recipe is an adaptation of the soft knotted bread that arrived in America with German immigrants in the early 19th century. The buns are unusual as the dough is poached prior to being baked, just like a bagel, and has a similar texture. These buns would be perfect for the German-inspired Currywurst dog (see page 9).

Makes 12 (ORDER UP! PAGE 61)

350ml/12fl oz/1½ cups milk
2 tbsp light brown sugar
7g/¼oz packet dry yeast
50g/2oz unsalted butter, melted
500g/1lb 2oz/4 cups strong white bread flour, plus extra for dusting
100g/3½ oz/scant ½ cup bicarbonate of soda (baking soda)
sea salt

Preheat your oven to 220°C/425°F/gas mark 7 and grease 2 large baking sheets.

In a small pan, heat the milk and sugar until tepid, then pour into the bowl of a stand mixer. Add the yeast, butter and flour and knead using the dough hook on a slow speed until the dough is smooth and elastic, about 10 minutes. Alternatively, combine the ingredients in a large bowl and work the mixture by hand, then knead on a lightly floured surface. Cover and leave in a warm place for about an hour or until doubled in size.

Divide the dough into 12 equal-size pieces, form into hot dog roll shapes and place on the greased baking trays. Bring 2.5 l/4½ pints/10½ cups of water to the boil in a large pan and add the bicarbonate of soda (baking soda). Poach the uncooked buns in the water for about 1 minute, turning so that both sides come into full contact with the water. Place back on the baking sheets and sprinkle with sea salt. Cut shallow slashes into the top of the buns. Put a roasting pan of water in the bottom of your oven to create some steam. Bake the buns for 12 minutes or until nicely coloured. Remove to a wire rack and allow to cool.

HOT DOG EATING COMPETITIONS

If you love hot dogs, and as you're reading this book, let's assume you do, then at some point in your life you're going to end up thinking the following thoughts: 'I can't get enough of those dogs, I could eat a whole plate of 'em in one go, after all they're only small. I should enter a hot dog-eating competition!' At the time, this will seem like a eureka moment, one of those few occasions in life when you've achieved real insight. You'll believe you've found the one thing you've been put on earth for. You are going to be rich. And then you find out about a man named Joey Chestnut.

On 4 July 2013, Joseph 'Jaws' Christian Chestnut stood on a stage in Coney Island, Brooklyn and, in front of an enthusiastic crowd of about 40,000 people and a television audience of millions, downed 69 hot dogs in 10 minutes to win the Nathan's Famous 98th Annual Hot Dog Eating Contest. That's one hot dog every 9 seconds.

In order to achieve that rate of consumption, Chestnut wasn't stopping to add mustard or sauerkraut to his dogs. Instead, his two-fisted method (and standard procedure in the competition) entailed chomping through two frankfurters at a time while simultaneously soaking a bun in a cup of water, squeezing out the soggy bread and forcing it into his mouth and dispatching it with a few bites. Meanwhile he soaked another bun, another squeeze, a few more bites and then two more sausages and so on. Fine dining it ain't.

In order to prepare, Chestnut told *The Hollywood Reporter* that he fasts for three days, drinking only gallons of water to stretch the capacity of his stomach which under normal circumstances simply wouldn't be able to hold that much food, then binges in a practice contest. Recovery from such an extreme diet takes up to 48 hours.

But for someone of Chestnut's appetite (the 6ft, 240 pound Californian is currently ranked number one in the world by the International Federation of Competitive Eating) it's worth the pain. For his 2013 efforts, Chestnut won $10,000 (that works out to about $145 per hot dog) and his seventh consecutive winner's yellow mustard belt. He's since gone on to win the competition again in 2014, but managed just 61 dogs. Perhaps his crown is slipping. Fancy your chances?

Relishes, defined as any cooked, pickled or chopped vegetable or fruit used to enhance the flavour of food, are a crucial part of the hot dog experience. No Chicago dog would be complete without sweet pickle relish (see page 74), for example, but there are dozens of other relishes served with dogs that are equally good.

At Flo's Hot Dogs in Cape Neddick, Maine, the sweet, spicy and sour onion relish is so well loved that it's available to buy by the jar to take away (you can even buy it on eBay). The recipe is 'secret' but probably contains onions, cabbage, cucumbers, molasses, vinegar, sugar, tamarind and chillies among its ingredients.

In Connecticut, they take their dogs seriously. So seriously that they even made a documentary about ten of the most famous stands in the state, called *A Connecticut Hot Dog Tour*. Included in the film is Blackie's, mostly unchanged since it opened in the 1930s and still serving their signature hot pepper relish. Another secret recipe that's been handed down through generations, it's a chunky sauce that packs heat, with both bell peppers and hot chilli peppers in the mixture.

In Philadelphia, your hot dog comes topped with pepper hash. An unusual but delicious concoction, it's a sort of pickled coleslaw and is made with finely chopped cabbage, green pepper and carrots marinated in a vinegar, sugar and salt solution.

The zucchini (courgette) relish at Snappy Dogs in Eastern Massachusetts may not have the sort of history behind it that Blackie's and Flo's has (the stand was established in 2010), but that doesn't stop it being just as delicious. Graduate of the Cordon Bleu culinary school, Lisa Volpe Hachey makes a whole range of unusual relishes including Moroccan carrot relish and watermelon rind chutney.

Across the southern States of America, you'll likely to be served chow chow with your dog. The ingredients of this mixed vegetable pickle can vary greatly, but might include green and red (bell) peppers, onions, green tomatoes and cabbage cooked in a sweet, sour and spicy mix of sugar, cider vinegar, mustard, chilli flakes, turmeric and ginger. Think of it as a transatlantic cousin to British piccalilli.

KETCHUP

MAPLE MUSTARD SAUCE

YELLOW MUSTARD

SWEET PICKLE RELISH

KETCHUP

Everyone loves ketchup, so imagine the kudos when you whip out your own homemade version at your next barbecue. It's a little time-consuming but not difficult at all, and will keep in a sterilized bottle in your fridge for up to a month.

Makes 1 litre/1¾ pints/4⅓ cups
(ORDER UP! PAGE 68)

1 tsp mixed peppercorns
1 clove
1 bay leaf
1 star anise
2 banana shallots, finely sliced
2 cloves garlic, minced to a fine paste
1 tsp Worcestershire sauce
1kg/2lb 4oz/scant 4¼ cups tinned chopped tomatoes
100g/3½oz/scant ½ cup tomato purée
150g/5½oz/scant ¾ cup light brown sugar
250ml/9fl oz/generous 1 cup cider vinegar
1 tsp Jamaican-style hot pepper sauce
1 tbsp sea salt

Put the peppercorns, clove, bay leaf and star anise in a square of muslin cloth and tie into a bag with kitchen string to make a bouquet garni. Place all the other ingredients in a large heavy-based pan and add the bouquet garni. Bring to boil, stir and leave to simmer over a low heat for an hour, stirring occasionally to prevent sticking. Allow to cool then blend with a stick blender and pass through a fine sieve back into a clean pan. Bring back to the boil and then simmer until the desired consistency is reached. Using a funnel, pour the still-hot sauce into sterilized bottles, cool, seal and refrigerate until needed. The ketchup will keep for up to a month in the fridge.

YELLOW MUSTARD

Of course you can buy yellow mustard, but making your own will give you a great sense of achievement and it's a piece of cake. Well, it's a pot of mustard actually, but you get the point. Another bonus to making your own is that you can tailor the level of spice to your own taste. Allow the mustard to mellow for a day or two before use.

Makes about 300ml/½ pint /1¼ cups
(ORDER UP! PAGE 68)

120ml /4fl oz/½ cup water
100ml/3½fl oz/scant ½ cup white wine vinegar
120g/4¼oz yellow mustard powder
1 tsp cornflour, slaked with 1 tsp of the water
1 tsp sea salt
½ teaspoon ground turmeric
½ teaspoon garlic powder
½ teaspoon paprika

Combine all the ingredients in a saucepan with 120 ml/4 fl oz/½ cup water. Bring to the boil over a medium heat, stirring continuously until the mixture thickens. Reduce the heat to a gentle simmer and cook for 10 minutes, stirring to prevent the mustard catching. Set aside to cool and transfer to a plastic squeezy sauce bottle. The mustard will keep in the fridge for several months.

MAYONNAISE, THREE WAYS

Emulsifying egg yolk and oil to make mayonnaise is one of the easiest, yet most satisfying, things you can do in a kitchen. It's used in a number of the sauces and sides in this book so it's a useful recipe to know, and once you realize how simple it is to make your own you'll never buy the bottled version again. Here's the base sauce recipe and two variations. The herb and garlic versions go particularly well with corn dogs (see page 22).

Makes 300ml/½ pint/1¼ cups
(ORDER UP! PAGE 69)

BASE RECIPE

3 medium egg yolks
2 tsp mild yellow mustard
2 tsp white wine vinegar
150ml/¼ pint/⅔ cup rapeseed (canola) or vegetable oil
lemon juice to taste
sea salt and white pepper

In the bowl of a stand mixer, or large mixing bowl, combine the eggs, mustard and vinegar and season with a pinch of salt and pepper. Dribble in the oil in a slow, steady stream, whisking constantly until you have a thick emulsion. Taste and adjust for seasoning and add a squeeze of lemon juice to brighten the flavours. Decant into a plastic squeezy sauce bottle. Apply at will to your hot dogs.

HERB MAYONNAISE

150ml¼ pint/²/₃ cup rapeseed (canola) or
    vegetable oil
1 small bunch of parsley, leaves picked from
    the stalks
1 small bunch of chives (about 12)
1 tbsp chopped tarragon leaves
3 medium egg yolks
2 tsp mild yellow mustard
2 tsp white wine vinegar
lemon juice, to taste
sea salt and black pepper

In a mini food processor, blend the oil with the parsley, chives and
tarragon. In the bowl of a stand mixer, or large mixing bowl, combine
the eggs, mustard and vinegar and season with a pinch of salt and
pepper. Dribble in the herb oil in a slow steady stream, whisking
constantly until you have a thick emulsion. Taste and adjust for
seasoning and add a squeeze of lemon juice to brighten the flavours.
Decant into a plastic squeezy sauce bottle.

GARLIC MAYONNAISE

3 medium egg yolks
2 tsp mild yellow mustard
2 tsp white wine vinegar
150ml¼ pint/²/₃ cup rapeseed (canola) or
    vegetable oil
4 cloves garlic, minced to a very fine paste
lemon juice, to taste
sea salt and white pepper

In the bowl of a stand mixer, or large mixing bowl, combine
the eggs, mustard and vinegar and season with a pinch of
salt and pepper. Dribble in the oil in a slow steady stream,
whisking constantly until you have a thick emulsion. Add
the garlic paste, stirring well to ensure it's evenly distributed
throughout the mayonnaise. Taste and adjust for seasoning
and add a squeeze of lemon juice to brighten the flavours.
Decant into a plastic squeezy sauce bottle.

SWEET PICKLE RELISH

This relish is essential for an authentic Chicago hot dog (see page 16). Commercial brands can sometimes be alarmingly verdant and overly sweet, so make your own and you'll be sure that you're eating all-natural ingredients that are sweetened to your taste.

Makes about 750 ml/1¼ pints/3 cups
(ORDER UP! PAGE 69)

3 cucumbers, peeled, deseeded and finely chopped
2 green (bell) peppers, destemmed, deseeded and finely chopped
2 onions, finely chopped
2¼ tbsp pickling salt
350g/12oz/1¾ cups caster (superfine) sugar

240ml/8fl oz/1 cup white wine vinegar
2 tsp coriander seeds
2 tsp yellow mustard seeds
1 tsp ground turmeric
1 tsp ground cumin
1 tsp English mustard powder
½ tsp dried chilli flakes (optional)

Combine the chopped vegetables in a large bowl, sprinkle over the salt and cover with cold water. Cover with cling film (plastic wrap) and leave at room temperature for about 2 hours, then drain and rinse well.

In a large pan, combine the sugar, vinegar, coriander seeds, mustard seeds, turmeric, cumin, mustard powder and chilli flakes (if using) and bring to the boil. Stir until the sugar has completely dissolved, then add the vegetables. Bring back to the boil, then simmer for 30 minutes, stirring occasionally until the mixture has thickened to a relish-like consistency. Spoon the hot relish into sterilized jars, seal, then leave to cool. The relish will keep for several months in the fridge.

MAPLE MUSTARD SAUCE

Sweet and piquant, this easy-to-make sauce tastes great with corn dogs (see page 22) or a hot dog simply adorned with some chopped onion or hot dog onions (see page 78). Make sure you buy pure maple syrup, which tastes far superior to blends made with added carob fruit syrup.

Makes 200ml/7fl oz/scant 1 cup
(ORDER UP! PAGE 68)

100g/3½oz wholegrain mustard
50g/2oz/¼ cup mayonnaise (see page 72)
3 tbsp maple syrup

Place all the ingredients in a bowl and stir well to combine. Refrigerate until ready to use.

CRISPY SHALLOTS

NEW YORK ONIONS

...HAN SLAW

CUCUMBER PICKLES

REMOULADE

CARAMELIZED ONIONS

This is a very simple recipe but it does take time and patience, as you'll need to keep an eye on the pan throughout the 30–45 minute cooking process. Best to switch on the radio and pour yourself a drink while you wait.

Serves 4

1 tbsp vegetable oil
2 large white onions, cut into 5mm/¼in slices
sea salt and black pepper

Put your largest frying pan or skillet over a medium-low heat and add the oil to heat. Tip in the onions and stir well to break the rings and coat with the oil. Cook gently for 30–45 minutes, stirring occasionally to prevent the onions from catching and burning. The onions are ready when they are tender and a deep golden-brown colour. Season with salt and pepper and serve. The onions will keep in the fridge in a covered container for about a week.

NEW YORK ONIONS

This is a take on the sort of onion sauce that's slathered over hundreds of dogs in the Big Apple every day. Cinnamon and maple syrup are listed as optional as, although they are commonly added items, they may not be to everyone's taste.

Serves 4 (ORDER UP! PAGE 76)

1 quantity of caramelized onions (see above)
2–4 tbsp ketchup (see page 70)
1 tsp mild chilli powder
2–3 drops of Tabasco sauce
1 pinch ground cinnamon (optional)
1 tbsp maple syrup (optional)

Put all the ingredients in a heavy-based pan and heat gently until combined, stirring continuously to prevent the onions from sticking. Serve hot.

CRISPY SHALLOTS

You'll find these shallots scattered over many salads throughout Southeast Asia, but they're fantastic on hot dogs and would be great on a grilled steak, too. They would usually be made with the small reddish shallots commonly found in Asia but you can use the larger banana shallot – a cross between an onion and a shallot. They are much easier to peel and slice and, as they are bigger, there aren't so many to deal with. The flavour, which is milder and sweeter than a standard onion, is just as good.

Serves 4 (ORDER UP! PAGE 76)

500g/1lb 2oz banana shallots, sliced and separated into rings
150g/5½oz/1½ cups plain (all-purpose) flour
3l/5¼ pints/13¼ cups vegetable oil, or enough to fill a countertop deep-fat fryer or a large heavy-based pan two-thirds full.
sea salt

Heat the oil to 180°C/350°F. Dredge the shallot rings in the flour. Tap off the excess and fry in batches until golden brown. Drain on kitchen paper and season with salt.

COLESLAW

Homemade coleslaw is so easy to make and is vastly better than the shop-bought stuff. Use good-quality, ready-made mayo if you're running short of time. This won't keep, so prepare your vegetables ahead of time and complete the recipe when you're ready to serve.

Serves 4 (ORDER UP! PAGE 76)

1 red onion, halved and finely sliced
¼ white cabbage, cored and finely sliced
1 large carrot, peeled and roughly grated
1 small bunch of parsley, leaves picked and finely chopped
4–6 tbsp mayonnaise (see page 72)
sea salt and black pepper
squeeze of lemon juice

Put the onion, cabbage, carrot and parsley in a large bowl and stir well to combine. Add 4 tablespoons of the mayonnaise and stir to coat all the vegetables, adding more if the mixture is too dry. Season to taste and add a squeeze of lemon juice to brighten the flavour. Serve immediately.

ASIAN SLAW

This spicy cousin to coleslaw is lighter as there's no mayo in the mix, and goes perfectly with any of the Asian-inspired dogs in this book.

Serves 4 (ORDER UP! PAGE 77)

½ Chinese cabbage, cored and finely sliced
1 daikon, peeled and coarsely grated
1 bunch of spring onions (scallions), trimmed and finely sliced on an angle
4 tbsp lime juice (2–3 limes depending on size and juiciness)
4 tbsp dark soy sauce
1 tbsp fish sauce
4 tbsp rapeseed (canola) oil
2 tsp toasted sesame oil
1 thumb-sized piece of fresh ginger, peeled and finely grated
1 jalapeño chilli, deseeded and very finely chopped
2 tsp toasted sesame seeds

Combine the cabbage, daikon and spring onions (scallions) in a large mixing bowl and toss together well. In a small bowl, combine the lime juice, soy, fish sauce and oils. Add the ginger and chilli and stir well. Pour over the vegetables and stir well to combine. You want the vegetables to be coated but not swimming in the dressing, so add a little at a time, as the amount needed will vary depending on the size of your vegetables. Sprinkle over the sesame seeds and serve immediately.

REMOULADE

This is really just coleslaw's fancy French cousin. Made with celeriac rather than cabbage, it has a lovely earthy flavour and its mustardy kick is just perfect with a classic New York dog. It also tastes great with charcuterie and smoked fish.

Serves 4 (ORDER UP! PAGE 77)

1 celeriac
200 ml/7fl oz/scant 1 cup mayonnaise (see page 72)
2 tsp Dijon mustard
1 tbsp fine capers, chopped
1 small bunch of parsley, leaves picked and finely chopped
sea salt and black pepper
squeeze of lemon juice

Trim and peel the celeriac and cut into thin matchsticks using a Japanese mandolin. If you prefer to use a knife, cut the celeriac into 5mm/¼in slices, then cut each slice into thin matchsticks. Alternatively, you can coarsely grate the vegetable, but the texture will not be as good.

Put 150 ml/¼ pint/⅔ cup of the mayonnaise with the mustard in a large bowl and combine with the celeriac until well coated. Add the remaining mayonnaise if the salad looks a little dry. Stir in the capers and parsley and season well with the salt, pepper and lemon juice to taste.

Allow to sit for around 30 minutes before serving to allow the celeriac to soften a little. The salad will keep for a day or two covered in the fridge.

CUCUMBER PICKLES

These sweet and tangy crunchy pickles are really easy to make and are addictively delicious. Particularly good served alongside a chilli cheese dog (see page 19), Sloppy Joe (see page 18) or barbecue dog with pulled pork (see page 52).

Makes 54 pieces (ORDER UP! PAGE 77)

3 cucumbers, peeled
6 tbsp sugar
2 tsp pickling salt or sea salt
125ml/4fl oz/½ cup white wine vinegar
1 bunch of dill, chopped
1 tbsp yellow mustard seeds
1 tbsp coriander seeds
3 bay leaves

In a large bowl, dissolve the sugar and salt in 225ml/8fl oz/scant 1 cup of hot water then add the vinegar. Allow to cool then add the dill, mustard, coriander seeds and bay leaves. Set aside.

Top and tail the cucumber and cut into three equal sections. Cut each in half lengthways and into three long wedges. Place in a shallow container, large enough to hold all the pieces without overlapping, and pour over the pickling liquid. Refrigerate for at least 24–48 hours (the longer the better) before use. The pickles will last for several weeks in the fridge.

MAKING A MEAL OF YOUR HOT DOG

A hot dog is a balanced meal in itself, composed of protein (the sausage), carbohydrate (the bun) and veggies in the form of onions, sauerkraut or one of the many other toppings suggested in this book. The only trouble is that it's a very small meal; a few bites and it's gone. In this section, we've suggested a few side dishes to add both interest and a little heft to your dog.

It has to be admitted that hot dogs aren't the healthiest foods on the planet, and none should be included as part of your slimming regime. Look on them as a delicious treat, an occasional meal to be eaten in moderation. Throughout the recipes in the book, there are serving suggestions for which sides will best complement each hot dog, but feel free to mix and match. If you want to fuse the Italian/American classic of mac 'n' cheese (see page 94) with the Korean kimchee dog (see page 32), no one will stand in your way.

There are plenty more ideas for making a meal of your hot dog that we haven't had the space to include in the book. Hot dog and soup would make an ideal lunch, perhaps a bowl of spicy black bean soup with the Mexican hot dog wrap (see page 33); a mug of warming mulligatawny to accompany the Indian chapatti hot dog wrap (see page 41) or an elegant chilled gazpacho to match the Spanish dog (see page 31).

For a lighter but still satisfying meal, a well-made salad will elevate your dog to best in class. Serve a classic New York or Chicago-style dog with that most American of creations, the Cobb salad made with egg, avocado, tomato, chicken, onion, bacon and blue cheese, which handily spells out E.A.T. C.O.B.B. if you forget to make a shopping list. (You just need to add some lettuce of your choice, but that would have spoiled the mnemonic.) Another light option would be a refreshing bulgar wheat tabbouleh salad made with lots of parsley with the Middle Eastern hot dog flatbread wrap.

Homemade baked beans will go down a storm with the barbecue dog, and why not complete the picture and serve the Sunday roast dog with some crunchy roast potatoes. Hold the overcooked Brussels sprouts, although finely shredded raw, they do make an excellent base for coleslaw.

ONION RINGS

CHILLI CHEESE FRIES

POTATO K

POUTINE

BACON RANCH FRIES

SKIN-ON FRIES

POTATO SALAD

HOT DOG MAC 'N' CHEESE

SKIN-ON FRIES

Double-cooking your fries might sound like a pain, but it's really only as much trouble as par-boiling potatoes before roasting them for Sunday lunch. For a rather boring and complicated reason, blanching the fries in oil at a lower temperature and then frying at a higher temperature produces a much crisper result and fries that won't go soggy the moment they hit the plate. There's nothing scientific about leaving the skin on, it just tastes great.

Serves 4 (ORDER UP! PAGE 87)

600g/1lb 5oz potatoes, washed
3l/5¼ pints/13¼ cups groundnut (peanut) oil (or enough to fill a countertop deep-fat fryer or a large pan ⅔ full)
sea salt

Cut the potatoes into 5mm/¼in-thick fries. Soak in water to remove excess starch and then dry thoroughly on kitchen paper. Line some baking trays with double layers of kitchen paper.

Bring the oil up to a temperature of 130°C/250°F (use a cooking thermometer to check the temperature if not using a deep fat fryer) and blanch the fries in batches for about 4 minutes, or until the oil stops bubbling. Transfer the fries to the paper-lined trays. The chips can now be cooled and kept in the fridge until you're ready to serve them.

Increase the temperature of the oil to 190°C/375°F and fry the potatoes for another 4 minutes, or until crisp and golden. Drain on kitchen paper, season with salt and serve immediately.

CHILLI CHEESE FRIES

This is a meal in itself, albeit not a very healthy one! The recipe makes about twice the amount of chilli you'll need, so keep the rest for when you make chilli cheese dogs (see page 19). Best served with homemade cheese sauce (see page 94 for method) with a portion of skin-on fries (see page 88) a scatter of chillies and 4 tablespoons of sour cream.

Serves 4 (ORDER UP! PAGE 86)

For the chilli
1 tbsp vegetable oil
1.25kg/2lb 12oz/ minced (ground) beef
1 large onion, diced
4 cloves garlic, minced to a paste
2 tsp ground cumin
1 tsp cayenne
2 tsp ground fennel seeds
1 tbsp smoked paprika
1 ancho chilli, reconstituted in water and diced
1 jalapeño chilli, seeds removed and finely diced
500ml/18 fl oz/2 cups beef stock
400g/14oz tin chopped tomatoes
400g/14oz tin black eyed beans
400g/14oz tin kidney beans
1 tsp cocoa powder
2 tsp dried oregano
sea salt and Tabasco sauce (optional)

For the cheese sauce
2 tbsp butter
2 tbsp plain (all-purpose) flour
2 tsp yellow mustard
500ml/18fl oz/generous 2 cups milk
175g/6oz Monterey jack cheese
sea salt and black pepper

To make the chilli, heat the oil in a large pan and fry the minced (ground) beef until browned, then transfer to a large bowl with a slotted spoon. Gently fry the onion in the same pan until soft. Add the garlic, cumin, cayenne, fennel seeds, smoked paprika and chillies. Return the meat to the pan and add the stock, tomatoes, beans, cocoa powder and oregano. Add water or more stock to cover the meat, if necessary, then bring to the boil and simmer gently for 2 hours. Adjust the seasoning with salt and Tabasco, to taste. Meanwhile, make the cheese sauce (see page 94). Preheat the oven to 200°C/400°F/gas mark 6. Transfer the fries (see page 88) to a large baking dish and pour over the cheese sauce. Heat until the cheese melts and begins to brown. Spoon over the chilli, scatter over the chillies and finish with the sour cream.

BACON RANCH FRIES

This dish is inspired by the version they serve at Nathan's Famous in Coney Island (see page 56). Buy good-quality dry-cure bacon that contains little or no added water, which will not only taste better than the standard stuff but will produce a crispier result, which is exactly what you need here.

Serves 4 (ORDER UP! PAGE 86)

For the ranch dressing
200ml/7fl oz/scant 1 cup mayonnaise (see page 72)
5 tbsp Greek yogurt
5 tbsp buttermilk
1 clove garlic, minced to a fine paste
1 small bunch of chives, finely sliced
1 pinch of cayenne pepper
squeeze of lemon juice
sea salt and black pepper

For the fries
8 rashers dry-cure streaky bacon
600g/1lb 5oz skin-on fries (see page 88)
1 small bunch of spring onions (scallions), trimmed and finely sliced at an angle

Make the ranch dressing by combining the mayonnaise, yogurt and buttermilk in a large bowl. Add the garlic, chives and cayenne and stir well. Season to taste with the salt, pepper and lemon juice, cover and leave to rest in the fridge for an hour.

Preheat the oven to 180°C/350°F/gas mark 4.

Lay the bacon on a rack over a lipped baking tray and transfer to the oven to cook for 15 minutes until crisp. Drain on kitchen paper, allow to cool, then chop into bite-sized pieces.

Prepare the fries as per the recipe, tip into a large serving bowl and toss through the bacon and spring onions (scallions). Pour over some of the ranch dressing and offer more at the table.

POTATO SALAD

Who doesn't love potato salad? Potatoes tossed in some decent mayo is a simple and wonderful thing, but the little extras included in this version elevate it into a different league. If you're up for some hot dog on hot dog action, why not slice up some cooked frankfurters and stir them into your salad?

Serves 4 (ORDER UP! PAGE 87)

500g/1lb 2oz new potatoes, peeled and halved
1 tsp sea salt, plus more for seasoning
1 tbsp white wine or white wine vinegar
5 tbsp mayonnaise (see page 72)
5 tbsp crème fraîche
1 tsp yellow mustard
1 pinch of cayenne pepper
1 tsp paprika
1 banana shallot, finely diced
1 small bunch of chives, finely sliced
squeeze of lemon juice

Put the potatoes in a large pan over a high heat and cover with water. Cover the pan and leave to cook until the water boils, then remove the lid and reduce the heat to a simmer. Add the salt and half cover the pan with the lid. Cook for 20 minutes, or until the potatoes are cooked through, but not too soft. Drain and return the pan to the heat for few seconds to drive off any residual water.

Tip the potatoes into a large mixing bowl and sprinkle over the wine or vinegar while the potatoes are still warm. When cooled, cut the potatoes into bite-sized pieces. Mix together all the remaining ingredients except the lemon juice in a small bowl, then pour over the potatoes. Mix carefully to coat the potatoes evenly but avoid breaking them up. Adjust the seasoning with salt and lemon juice and serve immediately.

POTATO KNISH

Knish is a baked or fried pastry usually filled with potato and onion. It arrived in North America around the turn of the 20th century, brought over by Jewish Eastern European immigrants. You'll find them on the menu of hot dog shops like Papaya King in New York and at some of the city's hot dog carts, although 90s public health legislation has made them much harder to come by on the street.

Makes 16 (ORDER UP! PAGE 86)

For the dough
125ml/4fl oz/½ cup tepid water
4 tbsp vegetable oil
1 tsp sea salt
1 tsp vinegar
250g/9oz/2½ cups plain (all-purpose) flour
1 tsp baking powder
1 egg, beaten
2 tbsp milk

For the filling
500g/1lb 2oz potatoes, peeled and cut into 1cm/½ in cubes
1 tsp sea salt
200g/7oz caramelized onions (see page 78)
1 small bunch of chives, finely chopped
sea salt and black pepper

To make the dough, combine the water with the oil, salt and vinegar in a mixing bowl. In a separate bowl, combine the flour and baking powder. Mix the flour into the wet ingredients until it forms a soft, slightly sticky dough. Allow to rest in the fridge for an hour. Bring a large pan of water to the boil. Add the potatoes and salt and cook for 10 minutes, or until the potatoes are cooked through. Drain and mash until smooth. Stir in the onions, chives, salt and pepper and allow to cool completely. Preheat the oven to 180°C/350°F/gas mark 4 and grease a large baking sheet. Mix the egg and milk together to make an egg wash. Divide the dough into 16 equal-sized pieces and roll each into a ball about 3cm/1¼in in diameter. On a floured surface, roll out each ball to form a thin disc, place a tablespoon of the filling mixture in the centre, then pull up the dough to encase it. Turn the knish over so the seam side is facing down and shape into a neat dome. Place on the baking sheet and brush over the egg wash. Repeat with the remaining dough, then bake for 25 minutes, or until golden brown. Serve warm.

ONION RINGS

These will be the most delicious onion rings you'll ever eat. It's all down to the beer and yeast that create a light, bubbly batter that fries to a crisp and crunchy carapace. For the purposes of this recipe, fizzy commercial lager works best, but feel free to experiment. Don't skip soaking the onions – it removes the harsh, raw flavours and helps to soften them up, so that when you cook them they'll be perfectly tender despite the brief cooking time. Feel free to add a pinch of your favourite spice to the batter if you like – smoked paprika, onion powder, garlic powder, cumin or cayenne pepper would all work well.

Serves 4 (ORDER UP! PAGE 86)

1 large white onion, sliced into 5mm/¼in-thick rounds
    and separated into rings
240ml/8fl oz/1 cup milk
225g/8oz/2¼ cups plain (all-purpose) flour
14g/½oz dried yeast
300ml/½ pint/1¼ cups lager
3l/5¼ pints/13¼ cups vegetable oil (or enough to fill a countertop
    deep-fat fryer or a large pan two-thirds full)
salt

Soak the onion rings in the milk for an hour. Meanwhile, make your batter by placing the flour and yeast in a large bowl and whisking in the lager until smooth. Set aside somewhere warm until needed.

Heat the oil to 180°C/350°F. Drain the onions and dip them into the batter to coat. Cook the batter-coated onions in batches for 3–4 minutes, or until golden. Remove onto kitchen paper to drain. Serve immediately.

HOT DOG MAC 'N' CHEESE

This substantial side could make a meal by itself with a green salad. If you're going to serve this with a hot dog and feel the inclusion of sausage is just too much of a good thing, simply omit them.

Serves 4, or 8 as a side dish
(ORDER UP! PAGE 87)

10g/¼oz table salt
300g/10½oz dried macaroni
2 tbsp butter
500ml/18fl oz/generous 2 cups whole milk
2 tbsp plain (all-purpose) flour
2 tsp yellow mustard
280g/10oz Cheddar cheese, grated
250g/9oz caramelized onions (see page 78)
8 hot dogs of your choice, cut into chunks
sea salt and black pepper

Preheat the oven to 180°C/350°C/gas mark 4 and lightly grease a large baking dish.

Bring a large pan of water to the boil. Add the salt, then tip in the pasta. Bring back to the boil, then reduce the heat and simmer until cooked through, about 8 minutes or as per packet instructions. Drain and transfer to the prepared baking dish.

Meanwhile, make the cheese sauce by melting the butter in a heavy-based pan. Add the flour and stir until combined and golden. Add the mustard, then gradually stir in the milk, allowing the sauce to thicken slightly between each addition. Bring to the boil, then simmer very gently for 20 minutes, stirring regularly to prevent the sauce catching. Remove the sauce from the heat and add 175g/6oz of the cheese, stirring until the cheese has completely melted. Season with salt and pepper to taste and keep warm.

Stir the caramelized onions into the pasta with the chopped hot dogs. Pour in the cheese sauce and stir to combine and coat the pasta. Scatter over the remaining cheese and bake for 20 minutes, or until browned and bubbling. Serve hot.

POUTINE

Before you say anything about this 1950s culinary creation from Quebec in Canada of fries, gravy and cheese, remember the last time you brought home chips with curry sauce from the chippy? I rest my case. Canadians make poutine with 'white cheddar cheese curds', a product not available outside of North America. Its closest cousin is not British cheddar but processed mozzarella in a block, which has less moisture than its fresh counterpart and is more able to hold its shape and not melt, making for a more authentically Canadian result.

Serves 4 (ORDER UP! PAGE 86)

600g/1lb 5oz skin-on fries (see page 88)
500ml/18fl oz/generous 2 cups gravy (see page 45)
200g/7oz processed mozzarella, diced into small cubes
sea salt

Bring the gravy to the boil and keep warm. Divide the fries between four serving bowls and season with salt. Pour over enough of the hot gravy to coat the fries. Divide the cheese between the four bowls and mix into the gravy-coated fries. Serve immediately.

A-Z

HOT DOGS

BBQ DOG WITH PULLED PORK 52

BLUE CHEESE AND BACON DOG 53

CHICAGO HOT DOG 16

CHILLI CHEESE DOG 19

CORN DOG 22

CURRYWURST 9

INDIAN CHAPATI HOT DOG WRAP 41

KOREAN KIMCHI DOG 30

MALAYSIAN SATAY DOG 32

MEXICAN HOT DOG WRAP 33

MIDDLE EASTERN HOT DOG 42

PHILLY CHEESE DOG 17

PIZZA DOG 54

PO' BOY 23

SLOPPY JOE DOG 18

SPANISH DOG 31

SUNDAY ROAST DOG 44

THAI DOG 40

BUNS, RELISHES, TOPPINGS & SIDES

ASIAN SLAW 81

BACON RANCH FRIES 90

BRIOCHE HOT DOG BUNS 62

CARAMELIZED ONIONS 78

CHILLI CHEESE FRIES 89

CRISPY SHALLOTS 79

COLESLAW 80

CUCUMBER PICKLES 83

HOT DOG BUNS 60

HOT DOG MAC 'N' CHEESE 94

KETCHUP 70

MAPLE MUSTARD SAUCE 75

MAYONNAISE, THREE WAYS 72

NEW YORK ONIONS 78

ONION RINGS 93

POTATO KNISH 92

POTATO SALAD 91

PRETZEL HOT DOG BUNS 63

POUTINE 95

SKIN-ON FRIES 88

SWEET PICKLE RELISH 74

REMOULADE 82

YELLOW MUSTARD 71